Cat Hill and Emma Ford

Photographs by
Mary Patricia Stone

THE KID'S GUIDE TO HORSEMANSHIP AND GROOMING

Everything You Need to Know to Care for Horses
While Staying Safe and Having Fun

Trafalgar Square
North Pomfret, Vermont

First published in 2022 by
Trafalgar Square Books
North Pomfret, Vermont 05053

Copyright © 2022 *Cat Hill* and *Emma Ford*

All rights reserved. No part of this book may be reproduced, by any means, without written permission of the publisher, except by a reviewer quoting brief excerpts for a review in a magazine, newspaper, or website.

Disclaimer of Liability
The authors and publisher shall have neither liability nor responsibility to any person or entity with respect to any loss or damage caused or alleged to be caused directly or indirectly by the information contained in this book. While the book is as accurate as the authors can make it, there may be errors, omissions, and inaccuracies.

Trafalgar Square Books encourages the use of approved safety helmets in all equestrian sports and activities.

Library of Congress Cataloging-in-Publication Data
Names: Hill, Catherine, 1981- author. | Ford, Emma, 1976- author. | Stone, Mary Pat, photograther.
Title: The kid's guide to horsemanship and grooming : everything you need to know to care for horses while staying safe and having fun / Cat Hill and Emma Ford ; photographs by Mary Pat Stone.
Description: North Pomfret, Vermont : Trafalgar Square Books, 2022. | Includes index. | Audience: Ages 5-12 | Audience: Grades 4-6 | Summary: "A kid-friendly introduction to safe and proper horse care from the best in the business. Whether taking their first lessons, handling horses when visiting friends, or enjoying the glorious challenges of first-pony ownership, children need to learn more than just "how to ride." When it comes to horses, the most important lessons begin on the ground, not only to ensure a young person's safety, but also to promote the fair and informed care of an animal so that he remains healthy and happy in their interactions, too. This highly illustrated, easy-to-use book is the most complete and correct guide available for horse-crazy kids and their families to learn basic horsemanship standards and responsibly apply them in the barn, in the arena, at home, and at competitions. Professional grooms and authors of the bestsellers World-Class Grooming for Horses and World-Class Braiding-Manes & Tails Cat Hill and Emma Ford are both lifelong horsewomen who have managed barns and strings of horses for top riders in all disciplines, including Olympians and World Champions. Since publishing their first book, they have traveled the country teaching clinics in proper horsemanship and grooming to aspiring young riders. Now they have put their wealth of experience to the page with over 800 professional color photos and clear, numbered steps that teach readers the following: catching, leading, and handling; daily grooming; tacking up; post-riding or lesson care; tack cleaning; barn chores; packing for shows and competitions; bathing, clipping, and braiding; bonding and playing; games and goals for those who don't want to show; and more!"-- Provided by publisher.
Identifiers: LCCN 2021049346 (print) | LCCN 2021049347 (ebook) | ISBN 9781646010820 (hardcover) | ISBN 9781646010837 (epub)
Subjects: LCSH: Horses--Juvenile literature. | Horsemanship--Juvenile literature. | Horses--Grooming--Juvenile literature.
Classification: LCC SF285.3 .H535 2022 (print) | LCC SF285.3 (ebook) | DDC 636.1--dc23/eng/20211012
LC record available at https://lccn.loc.gov/2021049346
LC ebook record available at https://lccn.loc.gov/2021049347
LC ebook record available at https://lccn.loc.gov/2021031900

Photos by *Mary Patricia Stone* except p. 2 (courtesy of the authors)
Book design by *Katarzyna Misiukanis–Celińska (https://misiukanis-artstudio.com)*
Cover design by *RM Didier*
Typefaces: *Source Serif Pro, Zooja Pro* and *Active*

Printed in China

10 9 8 7 6 5 4 3 2 1

This book is written for all the kids
who are hungry for knowledge,
who ask all the questions, and want to
know everything there is to know.
Keep learning, and someday,
write a book for us to learn from!

This book is also written with
enormous thanks to all the ponies
that have the patience to endure
all the antics of pony-mad kids and
instill the love of horses in them, because
without the ponies, there wouldn't be
any kids to ask the questions!

INTRODUCTION 1

CHAPTER 1 — page 5
Catching, Leading, and Handling Your Horse
How to Catch a Horse in the Field 7
How to Halter Your Horse or Pony 8
How to Halter a Tall Horse 10
How to Approach a Horse in the Stall 11
Leading the Right and the Wrong Way 12
What Not to Do When Leading a Horse 16
When to Tie, How to Tie, How to Cross-Tie 16

CHAPTER 2 — page 21
Barn Chores and Feeding
How to Clean a Stall 22
Cleaning the Aisle 24
Cleaning Bowls and Buckets 26
How to Roll a Lead Rope 27
How to Fold a Blanket 28
Feeding Tips 28

CHAPTER 3 — page 35
Daily Grooming
Grooming Kit 37
Safety First! 45

CHAPTER 4 — page 51
Getting Ready to Ride—Tacking Up
Saddle Up 53

CHAPTER 5 — page 61
Leg Care and Protection
Feeling for Leg Issues 62
Protective Boots 63
Post-Work Leg Care 67

CHAPTER 6 — page 71
Post-Workout Bathing
Bucket Rinsing 72
Bathing with a Wash Rack 74
Bathing without a Wash Rack 82
Light-Colored Horses 85
Cold or Below-Freezing Towel Bath 88

CHAPTER 7
Tack Cleaning
91

Bridle 92
Saddle 103
Girth 105

CHAPTER 8
Travel Preparation: Equipment and Trailer Loading
107

Packing 111
Pony Leg Protection While Traveling 113
Heads and Tails 118
Blanket or Cooler 119
Preparing to Load 120

CHAPTER 9
Care at a Show or Clinic
125

Unloading 126
Setting Up Equipment 128
Cooling Out 129
Things to Remember at One-Day Shows and Clinics 130
Stabling Overnight 131
Setting Up Equipment for Overnight 133

CHAPTER 10
Pony Glow Up
139

Clipping 140
Banging the Tail 142
Cleaning Manure Spots 143
Finishing Touches 144

CHAPTER 11
Professional Care
161

Veterinarians 162
Farrier 169
Horse Dentist 173

CARING FOR THE VILLAGE 174
THE PONIES AND HORSE KIDS IN THIS BOOK ... 175
LEARN MORE! 176

v

acknowledgments

from Cat

I cannot say enough thanks to my family, since this book was nothing if not a family effort. Thanks to my mom and dad for the countless hours spent nurturing my love of horses—and a shoutout to Dad who came to the book photo shoot to play the part he knows so well! Thanks to my kids who cheerfully help in the barn and happily agreed to be photographed. And thanks to Marcus, for always encouraging me to chase my dreams, even if that involves much more work for him.

Like every horsewoman, I would not be where I am today without so many professionals answering my millions of questions, educating me at every turn, barking at me when I got it wrong, and making me try again until I got it right. Thanks to all of them for guiding my path. I also have to thank the grooms I have known over the years for teaching me so much, for always having each other's backs, and for living the dream. Thanks to Emma for her friendship, horsemanship, and kindness.

We would not have ever written a single page if not for the encouragement and guidance of everyone at our publisher Trafalgar Square Books. Support small publishers, everyone—without them, many of us authors would never type a single letter, let alone get it to print.

Huge thank you to veterinarian Dr. Barb Mix and farrier Russ Young. They are not only great at their jobs, but it turns out they are excellent models, too! And to to our photographer Mary Pat Stone. Her photos make this book come to life, and her cheerful attitude during the shoot made sure the kids had fun doing it, even when we had to reshoot...and reshoot...and reshoot again. We're so grateful for your work!

Finally, thank you to the horses; to not only Misty, Rhaj, Saheer, Sinimin, Riven, River, Stormy, and of course, Nicki Henley, but to

Cat and Emma with photographer Mary Pat Stone

the countless others who have taught me, trusted me, and made me.

"Some people are shaped by footprints in the sand, others by hoofprints in their hearts. You and me, kid, we're the latter." — Tom Florio

from Emma

This book has come to fruition because of an amazing career with horses that began with my first ride on a Shetland pony named Georgie and led to me grooming at the top level of equestrian sports. There are so many people and ponies to thank who have encouraged me along the way…to be quite frank, I can't remember everyone's name, but I do remember faces, and I truly appreciate the time all put into teaching an eager-to-learn kid who was at times, I'm sure, annoying!

First and foremost, thanks has to be given to my parents, Ken and Barbara, for putting me on my first pony when I was barely out of diapers and instilling the work ethic in me needed to care for animals. To my grandad who taught me how to braid, drove me to shows, and always had a hug and a joke for me, no matter the outcome. (Nanny might not have found riding in your house funny, but you and I had a good giggle!)

My love of caring for horses was ignited and encouraged by my time spent in the Stevenstone and Torrington Farmers Pony Club, in North Devon, United Kingdom. There I made many great friends and created many memories that included amazing instructors, peers, and ponies.

A huge thank you to photographer Mary Pat Stone for working with me and with Cat on this project. They say, "Never work with children and animals," but because of your energetic smile and positive attitude, the photoshoots could not have gone better.

To Cat Hill, my partner in business and one of my closest friends…another book completed! Thank you for keeping the pressure on to keep going, thank you once again for taking the helm with technology, and thank you for being a true friend.

Last but certainly not least, I would be remiss not to thank my amazing equine partners in my early years: To Georgie, Ashley Sukina, Minn, StoryTime, and Sir Trooper—you were my best friends when growing up, you loved me unconditionally without fail, and you always taught me to be humble and kind throughout life. I am forever indebted to you all.

introduction

Two little girls grew up in different countries—one in a family with a history of horses and English riding traditions; one in a family on a working farm with all sorts of animals, including a few ponies. The English girl learned through Pony Club and rose through the ranks of young riders, showing and caring for horses. The American girl learned through 4-H and by reading all the books she could. Both girls found a love of the horse itself, deeper than any desire to ride, compete, or hang out with friends. They wanted to learn how to take better and better care of the horses that looked to them for food, safety, and friendship. It was this drive to know more that led both girls to pursue *grooming*—caring for all aspects of the horse—professionally. And this was what led them to eventually meet while each worked for a top-level event rider: the English girl for Phillip Dutton and the American girl for Mara DePuy.

We are those two little girls all grown up. Between us we have worked in almost every corner of the English-riding horse community. We wrote our first book about horse care—*World-Class Grooming for Horses*—because we saw a lack of education but not a lack of people who wanted to learn. That book led us to start teaching horsemanship clinics. As we travelled the country, we visited lots and

EMMA & CAT

Here we are as horse-crazy kids and as adults, still doing all we can to keep horses healthy and happy!

Fun fact: The pinto foal in the picture is Stormy, the pony who appears in many of the photos in this book. Stormy is now 35 years young. Every day with her is so, so special.

2

lots of barns: big barns, small barns, backyard barns, and the fanciest barns around. Everywhere we looked we saw kids eager to learn, with that spark of "wanting to know more" in their faces. We worked with plenty of great Pony Clubs and 4-H groups, but we also found many kids without access to those educational frameworks. Those clinics are what led us to *this* book. We wanted to write a book for *you*—our horses' future caretakers.

We hope that in this book you will find answers to all the questions you may have about caring for a horse or pony. We hope you try to learn a little bit every day so you can do the right thing for your "best friend." We promise the extra time you take will strengthen the bond between you.

You've already taken the first step to more knowledge by opening this book. Take the book to the barn, and don't be afraid to get the pages dirty. Remember that trying to do new things, or learning to do old things better, is messy! You may not see exactly what you want from your first braid, and your aisle may not be as clean as the one you see in the pages ahead the first time you try to sweep. Keep at it! Show off your attempts proudly…and then try again. Your horse will thank you for every effort.

Cat & Emma

chapter one

Catching, Leading, and Handling Your Horse

1

Catching, Leading, and Handling Your Horse

This chapter is going to cover basic day-to-day safety and skills so every trip to the barn can be productive and fun!

We'll start off at the beginning. Every barn visit has a purpose, and most of the time it involves horses or ponies. It's important to remember that without them, there is no reason for the rest of it! So, everything you do during your barn visits should have them in the front of your mind.

One item to help you keep organized is to keep a *Horse Care Diary*. Start by jotting down what you do each day and how your pony seems to you that day. The entry can be as simple as:

September 2:
Groomed, rode for 30 minutes. Stormy was great but a little lazy.

In this diary, you can write down when the farrier and veterinarian come, keep track of how much work your pony is doing, and figure out patterns in his behavior.

When you first get to the barn, it's important to set the tone for your day. Catching and leading your horse safely and smoothly is the first step to a successful day at the stable.

How to Catch a Horse in the Field

A field with several horses in it can be a dangerous place. Always be aware of what the horses are doing, and the "tone" o f the herd. Look out for upright heads, pinned ears, and tenseness.

☆**1** Although Ivy here, is in her stall and not in the field, she is demonstrating, "Stay away" with her pinned ears, white eyes, and tight lips."

☆**2 A–F** Always approach your horse heading toward his shoulder, not his face **(A)**. Approaching the head or face can push the horse away from you **(B)**. If the horse turns and *walks*

CHAPTER 1 / Catching, Leading, and Handling Your Horse

7

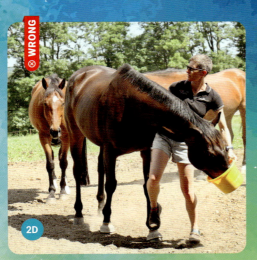

away, slowly, diagonally follow behind him—about a horse length or two. Do not walk directly behind him. Walking directly behind the horse can "push" him into a trot, and you are also in his "blind spot," which can lead to a kick. When he *trots* away, stop and stand until the horse stops trotting (or cantering), then quietly walk toward his shoulder again. If the horse lives outside alone, have a treat in your hand to reward him when he turns to you **(C)**. Be careful about carrying a bucket (such as one with feed in it) unless the horse is quite naughty to catch. A bucket can be difficult to handle and manage when a horse gets pushy or rude **(D)**. When there are several horses out together, avoid bringing a treat, but use a nice voice and a scratch on the withers when he stops. Quietly clip the lead rope under the chin if the horse wears a halter in the field **(E)**. Stormy is blind on this side, but you can see by her ears pointing at Quint that she has heard her name and is prepared to be caught. When the horse doesn't wear a halter, slip the lead rope over the neck, then hold both sides in one hand as you halter him **(F)**.

How to Halter Your Horse or Pony

☆ **3 A–D** Have your halter organized and ready. Note that carrying your halter like this will make it difficult to organize once you have

THE KID'S GUIDE TO HORSEMANSHIP AND GROOMING / Cat Hill & Emma Ford

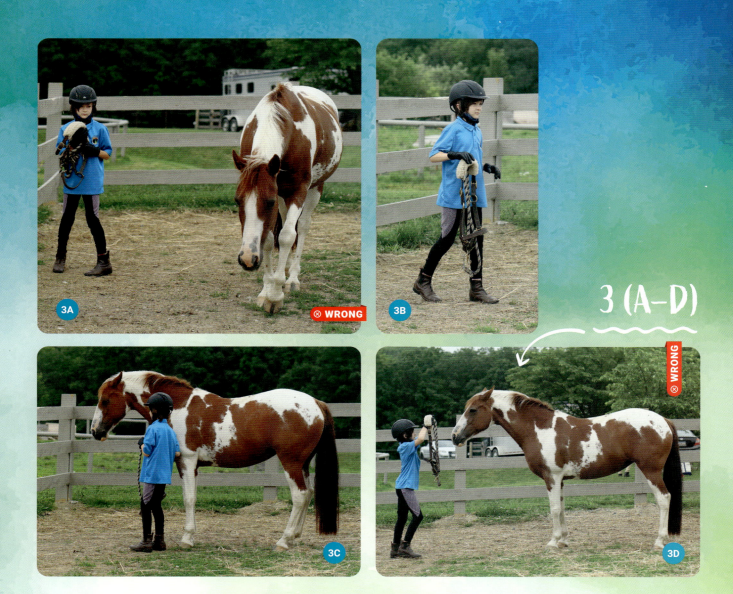

3 (A–D)

your pony near you **(A)**. With a buckle halter, undo the buckle, or a halter with a throat snap, undo the snap. Here, the halter is organized and with the lead rope ready to be put around Ivy's neck **(B)**. Approach your horse from a little to the side **(C)** and not directly in front of her nose **(D)**. Stand next to your horse's cheek on her near side. Open the nose area of the halter with one hand on each side.

☆ **4 A–D (next page)** If you are using a halter with a throatlatch snap, fold the crownpiece forward toward the noseband **(A)**. Carefully slide the halter over the horse's muzzle, then up and over her ears **(B)**. If you get stuck, a pat is always a good way to help your horse be patient **(C)**. Make sure to buckle the throatlatch; it can swing and hurt you or your horse when it's loose **(D)**.

CHAPTER 1 / Catching, Leading, and Handling Your Horse

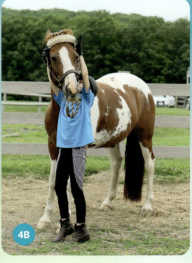

4 (A–D)

☆**5 A & B** When you have a halter with a buckle, slide the noseband high up the face, then push the strap of the crownpiece over the horse's neck well behind the ears **(A)**. Reposition the halter into the correct spot and buckle **(B)**.

How to Halter a Tall Horse

Sometimes a tall horse can be a bit of a trick to halter. Using a stool seems like a good idea until you are chasing a horse around a stall waiting for him to stand still long enough for you to set up the stool, get on, and get his head in the halter! Instead, you can teach a horse to come down to your level.

☆**6 A–F** First, approach the horse and give him a scratch or pat to say hello **(A)**. Slide the lead rope over the neck at the lowest point, near the withers **(B)**. Quietly give the

5 (A & B)

THE KID'S GUIDE TO HORSEMANSHIP AND GROOMING / Cat Hill & Emma Ford

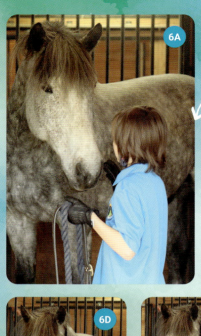

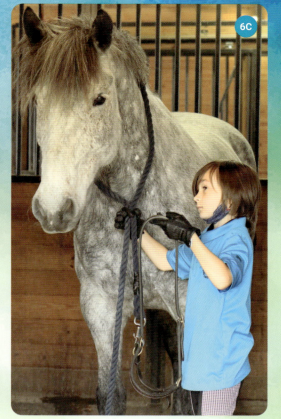

6 (A–F)

"Whoa" command as you reach around to the other side and grasp the tail end of the lead rope **(C)**. Standing next to the horse's neck on the near side, gently pull down on the rope and clearly say, "Head down" **(D)**. If the horse does not respond, shimmy the lead rope up the neck a bit and try again. Repeat this until the horse responds to the pressure by lowering his head **(E)**. If you have a horse who is very confused, have a helper hold treats very low to link the verbal command to the correct response. Once you have the horse's head lowered, quietly slide the halter on as described above **(F)**.

How to Approach a Horse in the Stall

☆ **7 A–E** A horse can feel trapped or scared if you go into his stall and surprise him. The goal is to have a horse come to you safely. First, open the stall door and greet the horse: "Hi, Stormy!" **(A)**. Next, close the door behind you so you can push it to exit but there isn't an escape visible to the horse. If the horse is facing you, go on to the next step. If the horse is facing away from you, cluck to him and ask him to move until he is facing you or is parallel to you. If clucking doesn't work, swing the lead rope in a circle and cluck a bit louder until he moves **(B)**. With your eyes looking at his shoulder, walk toward it, keeping your hands at your sides or slightly in front of you, palms up, but *not*

CHAPTER 1 / Catching, Leading, and Handling Your Horse

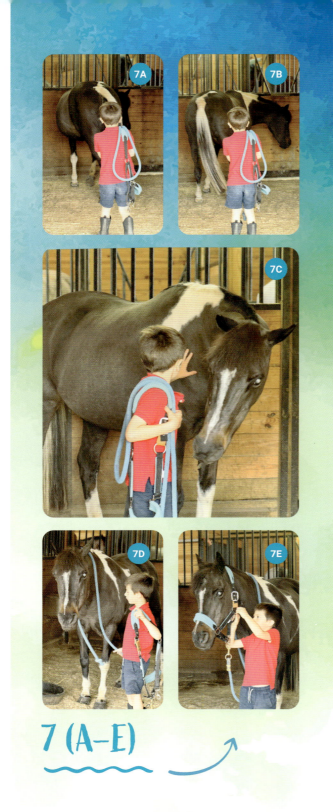

7 (A–E)

reaching out with Zombie arms as if to grab him! As you get close enough to touch him, start with a soft pat or scratch in front of the withers **(C)**. Slide the lead rope over his withers **(D)**. Halter him, or clip a lead rope while facing the same direction as the horse, rather than from in front of him **(C)**.

Leading the Right and the Wrong Way

When leading a horse or pony, always be very aware of your surroundings. You might have the most docile horse but there is no accounting for the unexpected to happen. A gun shot, a clap of thunder, a garbage can getting blown over—all can spook the quietest of horses.

Always have both hands on the lead rope. One hand should be approximately two-hands-width below the rope's clip. The second hand should be closer to the end of the lead rope ensuring there is no slack that can get tripped over or stood on.

☆ **8 A & B** Extra rope should be folded over in your second hand **(A)** and not wrapped around your hand **(B)**.

☆ **9 A & B** This rope has too much slack; it would be easy to trip over it. Glenn is also holding too close to the snap, and he could easily pull Stormy on top of him accidentally **(A)**. Here, the problems have been fixed **(B)**.

THE KID'S GUIDE TO HORSEMANSHIP AND GROOMING / Cat Hill & Emma Ford

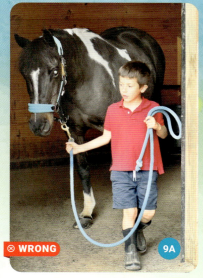

10 (A & B)

9 (A & B)

8 (A & B)

☆ **10 A & B** The grip of the rope should not be putting any pressure on the halter. Too tight **(A)**! This is better **(B)**.

☆ **11 A & B (next page)** When leading, position yourself on the near side (the horse's left), slightly behind the head but in front of the shoulder. Too far ahead **(A)**. Better **(B)**! When your horse doesn't automatically walk with you when asked, use your voice to encourage him—a quiet "cluck" will ask him to pay attention to what you would like him to do.

CHAPTER 1 / *Catching, Leading, and Handling Your Horse*

13

11 (A & B)

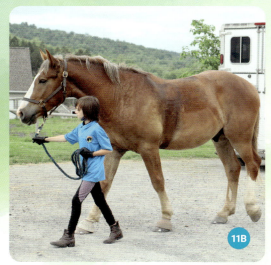

12 (A & B)

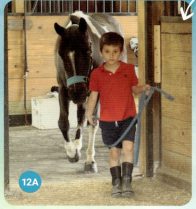

☆ **12 A & B** Whether going through a field gate or stall door, always make sure the space is wide enough for both you and the horse to walk through together **(A & B)**. Check for any latches that could get caught on the lead rope or hurt your horse if he spooks and bumps into them. Make sure your horse is completely through the gate or door and has plenty of space to turn around.

☆ **13** Remove the halter only when you have turned the horse around facing the gate ensuring that the exit is closed to prevent your horse from escaping.

☆ **14 A–J** Some horses require using a chain shank to ensure safety and control. Chain shanks can be dangerous to the horse so use with caution. They should be threaded through the halter's bottom ring, then the left-side square ring **(A)**. Next, wrap it over the top of the nosepiece, and out the other side's square ring **(B)**, and up to the high round ring, with the clip facing in, toward the horse's cheek **(C)**. A chain hooked just over the nose can break the delicate bones in the horse's face **(D)**. If you happen to have a chain shank, and do not want the chain to be in action as a corrective

THE KID'S GUIDE TO HORSEMANSHIP AND GROOMING / Cat Hill & Emma Ford

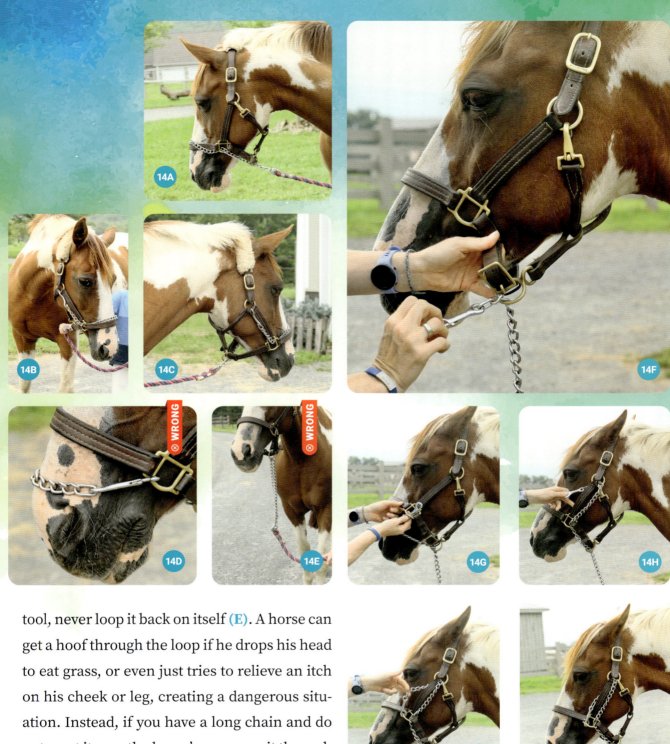

tool, never loop it back on itself **(E)**. A horse can get a hoof through the loop if he drops his head to eat grass, or even just tries to relieve an itch on his cheek or leg, creating a dangerous situation. Instead, if you have a long chain and do not want it over the horse's nose, run it through the bottom ring **(F)** up through the square ring on the side of the halter **(G)**, then down through the top round ring **(H)**, finishing by clipping it to the square ring on the side **(I)**. This

14 (A–J)

CHAPTER 1 / Catching, Leading, and Handling Your Horse

gives you a safer length of rope to hold, without putting the chain over the horse's nose (J).

What Not to Do When Leading a Horse

☆ **15** Never be on the phone when leading a horse.

☆ **16** Do not lead with one hand (always have both hands on the lead rope).

☆ **17** Never wrap the lead rope around your hand or wrist in any way.

☆ **18** Do not pull your horse along.

☆ **19** Do not let your horse drag you.

☆ **20** Always walk through the gate or door *with* your horse; never allow him to pass through ahead of you.

When to Tie, How to Tie, How to Cross-Tie

We need to tie horses for grooming, bathing, tacking up, the farrier, or at a show. It is important to understand that some horses have a fear of being tied or have never been taught. If you are working with a new horse, always be cautious about this step.

☆ **21** No matter where you tie, the rope or cross-ties should always be connected to some form

THE KID'S GUIDE TO HORSEMANSHIP AND GROOMING / Cat Hill & Emma Ford

of breakaway attachment. Note, this type of snap still needs to be tied to twine, since it requires a person to release it. This can be string, yarn, or baling twine. Due to the **strength of baling twine, unraveling several strands makes a better breakaway option.**

☆ **22** Breakaway halters have a little piece of leather designed to break under pressure; they are also a great choice whenever you are tying a horse.

Tying

It is important to practice tying your horse in an enclosed area before trying to tie him to an open tie rail or trailer for the first time.

☆ **23 A–F** To teach a horse to tie, first teach him to stand without tying a knot. Using a breakaway, just loop the rope through the attachment. Do not tie **(A)**. Go about your routine; if your horse steps back from the wall, ask him quietly to take a step forward every time he moves back. Repeating this pattern will teach him not to move away from that spot. Once he is comfortable with this, tying him with a quick release knot is your next step.

23 (A–F)

How to Tie a Quick Release Knot

☆ First, put the rope through the twine or breakaway **(B)**. Then cross the rope in front of itself to make a loop, fold the lower part of the rope and push the fold through the loop you made **(C & D)**. Pull the fold snug **(E)**. When there is an emergency, you can pull the tail

CHAPTER 1 / *Catching, Leading, and Handling Your Horse*

17

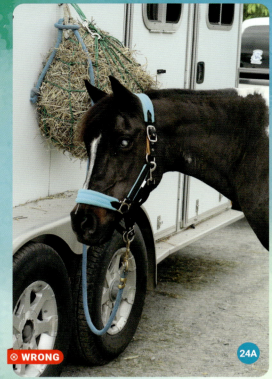

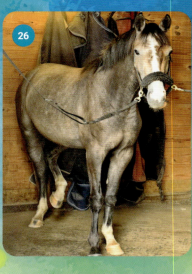

24 (A & B)

and the horse will be released **(F)**. Once your horse is happy to tie quietly in a stall, moving to outside locations such as trailers and hitching posts is the next step.

☆ **24 A & B** Stormy is tied too *loosely*; she could get a foot through the rope **(A)**. Stormy is tied too *tightly*; she cannot lower her head to a comfortable position **(B)**.

☆ **25** Using a hay net while tying to a trailer is useful in helping to keep your horse quiet. Always ensure the hay net is tied high enough to prevent a foot from getting caught in the net. Make sure you tie your hay net to twine or a breakaway just in case your horse gets caught up in it. Never leave your horse alone while tied.

Cross-Tying

☆ **26** Where possible, use cross-ties where the horse has three walls or rails surrounding him—two sides and one back. The back wall helps to prevent the horse from creating pressure on the top of his head (poll) that can cause him to fight and try to run backward.

THE KID'S GUIDE TO HORSEMANSHIP AND GROOMING / Cat Hill & Emma Ford

☆ **27 A–H** When walking into cross-ties, allow the horse to look and touch what is at the back of them so he understands what is behind him **(A & B)**. The cross-ties should never be tight when the horse is standing in the center of the area or so loose that the horse can touch the ground **(C & D)**. There should be enough slack to create a shallow loop **(E)**. Always pay attention to the horse's attitude. A lot of moving from side to side or back and forth show signs of a nervous horse. If possible, have a helper hold your horse in the area without tying him up to allow him to settle. Stormy has wiggled so far toward the wall and put Gwen in a potentially dangerous position. Because she isn't cross-tied though, Emma can simply walk her forward or back her up to get back to safety **(F)**. Once your horse is quiet, put him on the cross-ties, keeping the helper next to him should he need to be removed from the ties. Here, Stormy has quieted down but keeps shifting to the side. GG quietly asks her to move her hip over by gently pushing on her hindquarters **(G & H)**. Cross-tying is a learning experience that can take time and patience. If you are lacking time, use the horse's stall to complete the task safely.

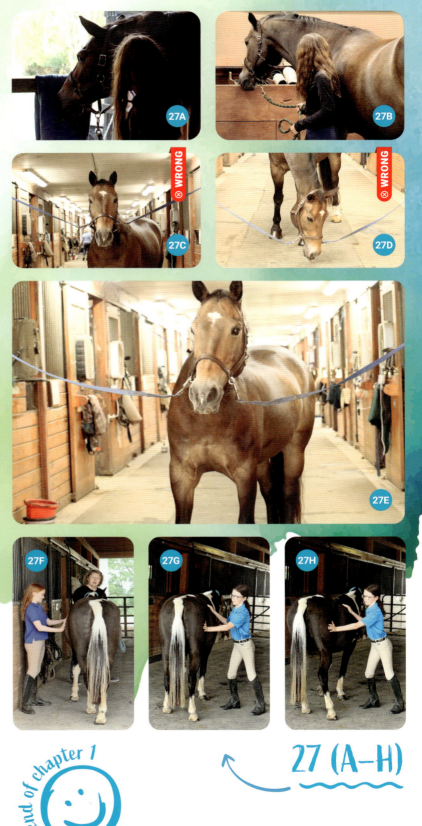

CHAPTER 1 / *Catching, Leading, and Handling Your Horse*

chapter two

Barn Chores and Feeding

2

Barn Chores and Feeding

Barn chores are an important but often tedious part of owning and riding horses! It is important that we remember that without our care, the ponies cannot stay healthy and happy. All barns should be kept as tidy as possible, for both the horses' safety and your own.

I like to make the chores fun by setting challenges: How fast can I clean a stall, what patterns can I make in the aisle with my rake? The amount of care a horse or pony needs depends on a lot of factors. A pony that lives inside a stall most of the day needs it cleaned more often than one that is outside for a longer period of the day.

How to Clean a Stall

Remember, a stall must be kept very clean. A dirty stall can make your pony sick because it invites flies, smells bad (which can cause damage to his breathing), and can make his feet rot. A stall should be cleaned at minimum once every twelve hours a pony is in it.

☆**1** To clean a stall, first make sure you have a pitchfork that fits you. There are several great options for youth-sized pitchforks, some have a full basket and others are flatter. The full basket is great for learning so you don't lose the poop you have worked so hard to pick up.

☆**2 A–I** Clean all the big piles off the top of the shavings or bedding **(A)**. Next, start at the left front corner of the stall and pick up a scoop of bedding **(B)**. Throw the shavings up along the edge of the stall, making a little pile of bedding along the wall **(C)**. Manure will roll to the bottom of your pile. Lift it out **(D)**, and shake your pitch fork to separate the manure from the clean bedding **(E)**. When you hit areas that

CHAPTER 2 / Barn Chores and Feeding

23

1 (G–I)

are heavy to pick up, turn them over in the bare spot on the floor, and if the bedding is wet (wet bedding is darker, reddish, and shiny), remove it **(F)**. Work your way all around the stall until the center is empty and clean and the bedding is piled all along the walls. Now, turn your pitchfork over and rake the bedding from the walls back toward the center **(G)**. Smooth it out nice and flat **(H)**, but keep it slightly deeper near the walls to prevent the pony from getting stuck against the wall if he rolls (this is called "getting cast"). Now, sweep or rake the front of the stall back so the horse has a nice clean area where he eats **(I)**.

Cleaning the Aisle

The aisle should be swept or raked to prevent the buildup of hay, dirt, and shavings. When this isn't done regularly it can lead to dangerous conditions like mold and rodents.

☆**3 A–F** To rake, start on one side of the aisle. Use short, powerful strokes to drag the rake across the dirt parallel to the walls **(A)**. Walk across the aisle making sure to get the whole area. Then start your way back **(B)**. Work back and forth all the way down the length of the aisle. You can have a little fun and rake patterns in the aisle for your friends to find **(C)**. To sweep, find a broom that fits you! Now, hold the broom fairly upright and use short strokes to sweep across the dirt **(D)**. Move back and forth from

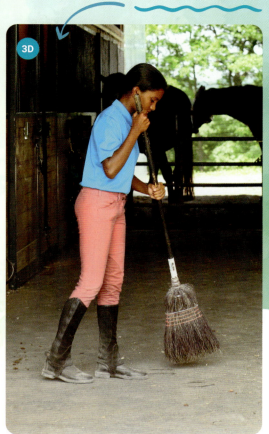

3 (A–F)

CHAPTER 2 / Barn Chores and Feeding

25

4 (A & B)

right to left, making sure you catch all the little stray bits **(E)**. Work your way all the way down the aisle, then sweep the dirt into a large pile near the wall. Lean your shovel against the wall and sweep your pile onto it **(F)**. Lay your broom against the wall and carefully pick up your shovel and dump the dirt into the manure pile or wheelbarrow.

Cleaning Bowls and Buckets

☆**4 A & B** Water buckets should be emptied and scrubbed **(A)**, then put back into place with fresh clean water **(B)**. Feed bowls should be cleaned out regularly, and troughs should be dumped and scrubbed periodically too. If you keep your horse at a boarding barn, ask the manager or owner what you can do to help keep the barn tidy!

☆**5** You should never leave a mess in the aisle—it's unsafe and unsightly.

THE KID'S GUIDE TO HORSEMANSHIP AND GROOMING / Cat Hill & Emma Ford

☆**6** Dirt should be swept up and halters hung neatly from hooks.

How to Roll a Lead Rope

☆**7 A–F** Rolling a lead rope takes a little practice, but it is a safer way to store lead ropes because there aren't loops to catch a horse's foot. Hold the clip end of the lead rope in one hand, and make a short loop **(A)**. Next starting at the clip end, take the remaining rope and twist it around the loop heading away from the clip. These twists should be as tight as you can make them **(B)**. After a few twists, push them in one motion up toward the clip **(C)**. Keep twisting until you only have a short amount of rope left and a small part of the loop open **(D)**. Now take the rope and push it through the loop—but not *all* the way **(E)**. When you need to release the rope, you can just hold the clip and pull the end, and the rope will unravel easily and quickly **(F)**.

CHAPTER 2 / Barn Chores and Feeding

27

☆**8** Cobwebs are a fire hazard, especially near lights. Every barn always needs cobwebs removed, so you can always offer to help out there!

☆**9** Speaking of fire hazards, it's a good idea to have a fire extinguisher near the door of the barn.

How to Fold a Blanket

☆**10 A–L** Folding blankets to keep them off the floor is ideal to keep aisles clear of clutter. You decide which is tidier **(A & B)**. The easiest way to fold light sheets and blankets is to find a swept area of the barn where you can fold the blanket on the ground **(C)**. Holding the blanket at the top of the neck, then at the top of the tail end, fold the blanket in half **(D–F)**. Now take the neck end and fold toward the tail **(G & H)**. Think about a burrito and how it gets folded in thirds. Take the bottom edge of the blanket and fold to the center **(I)**. Any straps can be slipped inside the blanket **(J)**. Now repeat the fold, this time with the opposite side of the blanket **(K & L)**. Pick up the bundle in the center **(M)**. Place the open tail end over the blanket bar **(N)**. Make sure the blanket lies flat over the bar **(O)**. The tidy straight edge of the blanket should be in the front **(P & Q)**.

Feeding Tips

Hay

Feeding horses is a complicated business. Every pony is different and what suits one pony really

ERRATA

The Kid's Guide to
HORSEMANSHIP AND GROOMING

PAGE 28

How to Fold a Blanket

☆**10 A–L** Folding blankets to keep them off the floor is ideal to keep aisles clear of clutter. You decide which is tidier **(A & B)**. The easiest way to fold light sheets and blankets is to find a swept area of the barn where you can fold the blanket on the ground **(C)**. Holding the blanket at the top of the neck, then at the top of the tail end, fold the blanket in half **(D)**. Now take the neck end and fold toward the tail **(E & F)**. Think about a burrito and how it gets folded in thirds. Take the bottom edge of the blanket and fold to the center. Any straps can be slipped inside the blanket **(G & H)**. Now repeat the fold, this time with the opposite side of the blanket **(I & J)**. Pick up the bundle in the center. Place the open tail end over the blanket bar **(K & L)**. Make sure the blanket lies flat over the bar. The tidy straight edge of the blanket should be in the front.

10 (C-L)

CHAPTER 2 / Barn Chores and Feeding

11 (A–C)

well may not work for his neighbor. It is important to have an adult with training help you create a diet for your pony. Your trainer, barn manager, or veterinarian are good people to turn to for help.

All diets should be "forage first." Forage refers to hay or grass. This is what horses and ponies digest the most easily and what nature designed them to eat. Lots of dry, clean hay should be available anywhere grass is limited.

☆**11 A–C** Hay nets with smaller holes can help keep greedy horses from eating their hay up too quickly and make sure they have hay in front of them all day, which is better for them **(A)**. Hay nets should always be hung from baling twine so they can breakaway easily should a horse get stuck in the net. Hay feeders ensure hay stays dry and clean outside **(B & C)**.

☆**12 A–C** Knowing what type of hay your pony eats is important. The basic types are *grass* hay

THE KID'S GUIDE TO HORSEMANSHIP AND GROOMING / Cat Hill & Emma Ford

30

and *legume* hay. Grass hay is generally high in fiber and low in sugar. Timothy, coastal, and orchard are all types of grass hay **(A)**. They make up most of a horse's diet. *Legume* hay is alfalfa, or in some areas, peanut hay **(B)**. Legume hay is high in protein and has more nutritional value per pound. It can be "rich," so should be used for specific purposes, like for older, in heavy work, or thin horses. Ideally, you should feed hay by weight, because how big a flake size can be very different depending on the type of hay and baling equipment used. When you first get a load of hay, take one flake, tie a piece of string around it, then use a hanging scale to weigh it **(C)**. A decent range for a horse is 15 to 20 pounds of hay per day, but this is a very rough estimate and can vary widely depending on each individual horse.

Grain

Grain products can provide extra calories for horses and ponies that need them. They should be added to the diet as needed, and the quantity may have to be changed frequently, depending on the ponies' work.

☆**13 A–C** *Hard grains* refer to either whole-plant seeds like corn and oats, or processed grains that are mixed by a feed company **(A)**. Many grains, like this beet pulp, must be soaked in water before being fed **(B & C)**.

12 (A–C)

CHAPTER 2 / Barn Chores and Feeding

31

13 (A–C)

Supplements

Supplements are added to the diet to make sure a pony gets all the nutrients he needs. Common supplements are *electrolytes*, which are minerals to help the horse stay hydrated and direct his body to drink enough water. *Vitamins* help the horse that is not getting enough of them from forage. For instance, many horses in the Northeast need vitamin E because the hay in this region is often low in it. *Balancers* are a complete vitamin that gives a little of everything to keep a horse feeling his best. *Oils* have fatty acids that are necessary for many vitamins to be absorbed.

☆ **14 A & B** Supplements should be added carefully, with the scoop close to the bucket to prevent it from sprinkling on the ground instead of the grain **(A)**. Then it should be mixed in with the grain. A wooden spoon, garden trowel or sweat scraper all work as mixers, but it should be used only for mixing feed **(B)**.

14 (A & B)

THE KID'S GUIDE TO HORSEMANSHIP AND GROOMING / *Cat Hill & Emma Ford*

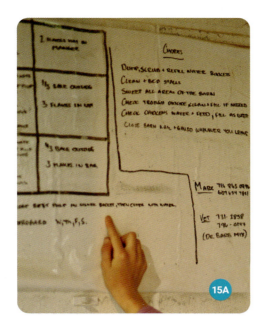

☆**15 A–E** Every barn should have a feed chart with clear instructions explaining what each horse gets **(A)**. Refer to this chart whenever you help make feed up for the horses. Hard grains should be fed by weight. It helps to have a scoop for each type of grain. You can weigh the amount needed **(B)** and draw a clear line on the scoop, which is an easier way to feed the correct weight every day **(C)**. When making grain, it's useful to have a bucket labeled for each horse **(D)**. Then, you can make feed ahead of time and know that each horse will get the correct feed and extras **(E)**.

☆**16** Salt blocks should be provided for every horse.

15 (A–E)

end of chapter 2

CHAPTER 2 / *Barn Chores and Feeding*

33

chapter three

Daily Grooming

3

Daily Grooming

*So why do we groom our ponies?
Having a clean pony prior to putting on tack
or blankets is very important;
however, a daily groom is also necessary
to keep your pony's skin and coat healthy
and free from any irritations
that could cause a problem.*

The time you spend grooming allows you to form a friendship with your pony as you notice his reactions to where and how you brush. Your pony may not "say anything" out loud, but a flick of an ear, swish of the tail, relaxed muzzle, or droopy lip are all signs of "horse talk." As you go through the grooming routine, watch out for your pony telling you that you might be brushing too hard, or he would like a longer groom in certain areas.

☆**1 A–E** Wesley turns his head with a soft eye to say, "That feels nice." **(A)**. Ivy says she does not like that **(B)**. Greyson gives a snuggle in return for some currying **(C)**. Pawing can mean, "I'm uncomfortable or unhappy" **(D)**. Kicking can mean many things: "I hate that," "I hurt," or simply, "I hate the bugs!" **(E)**.

1 (A–E)

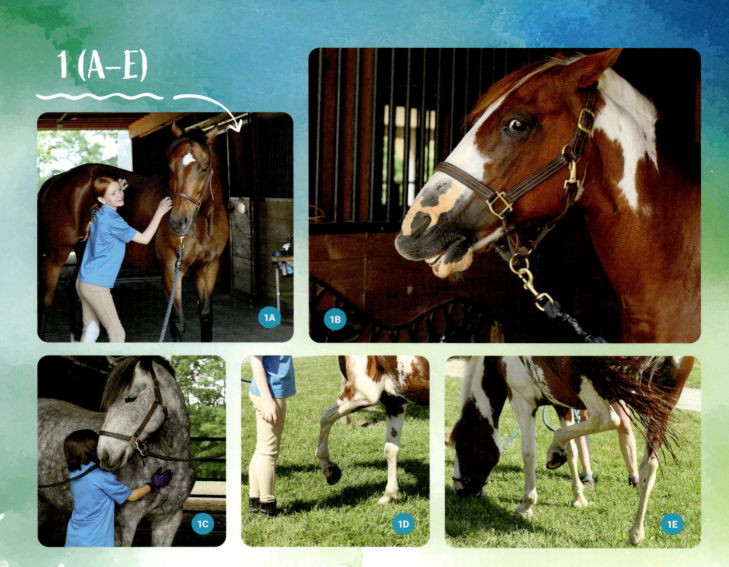

Grooming Kit

Curry Comb

Currying is one of the most critical parts of the grooming routine. It lifts dirt and dander from the skin and undercoat, and brings it all to the surface.

There are many types of curry combs, from the softest cactus cloth to a stiff metal comb. Your horse will tell you which curry comb he likes best—horses have different comfort levels.

☆ 2 A–D Start at the horse's shoulder and rub the curry in a circular motion, or across the grain of the hair (A). Take note of any attitude changes in your pony. Here, we are using a Posture Prep curry on Greyson, which is both a grooming and massage tool (B). On some areas, your pony will want to be curried harder—generally the crest or withers. This mimics how wild horses groom each other in natural settings. However, use less pressure across his spine and flanks as these areas can be sensitive. Wesley throws his head, flicks his tail and stomps when too much

CHAPTER 3 / Daily Grooming

pressure is used on his back **(C)**. Faces and legs should be curried, but make sure to use a soft rubber curry in these places **(D)**.

Long Bristle Stiff Brush (Dandy Brush)

☆**3 A–C** You use this brush in short, flicking strokes to remove the dirt and dander made visible using the curry **(A)**. To help keep the brush clean, you can use the curry to clean the dandy brush as you go **(B & C)**. Try to get into a pattern of brushing three strokes with the dandy brush then two strokes with the curry comb. You can use this brush all over your pony's body, but on his head, use lighter pressure and be careful not to brush over his eyes because the bristles can scratch his eyes and cause damage.

Short Bristle Soft Brush (Body Brush)

☆**4 A–C** This brush can be used in long strokes, following the direction of the hair **(A)**. Make sure to brush the head, following the direction of the hair **(B & C)**. Use the curry comb to clean the same way you did the dandy brush.

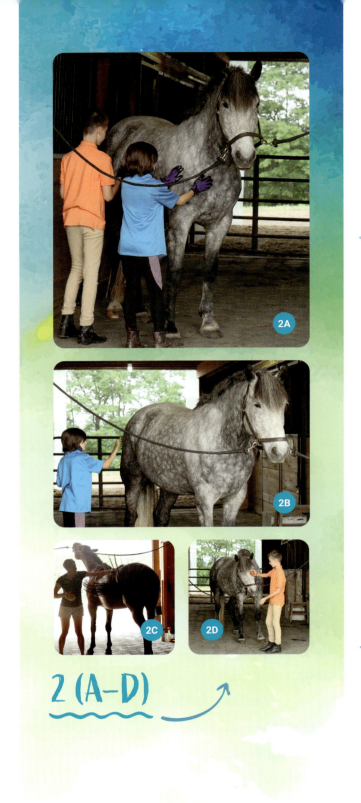

2 (A–D)

THE KID'S GUIDE TO HORSEMANSHIP AND GROOMING / Cat Hill & Emma Ford

38

3 (A–C)

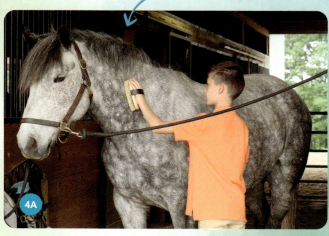

4 (A–C)

5 (A & B)

Towel or Sheepskin Mitt/Conditioner

You have a couple of options to finish grooming the body:

☆ **5 A & B** Wet a *towel* in warm water and wring it out as dry as you can **(A)**. Wipe your pony from head to toe; occasionally, turn the towel to a cleaner spot **(B)**.

CHAPTER 3 / Daily Grooming

39

PRO TIP
Products That Help Small Hands

♡ <u>HandsOn® Grooming Gloves</u>: These come in small sizes and are really helpful in your grooming session because you don't have to both hold onto a curry comb and apply pressure. Your hands do the grooming for you!

♡ <u>Epona Curry Brush™</u>: This is great for the sensitive face and legs.

♡ <u>Ultimate Hoof Pick</u>: The Jackhammer Junior: This really fits small hands well and breaks through hard dirt without the need for grown-up muscles.

♡ <u>Leistner "Prinz" Brushes</u>: These are the perfect size and texture to finish the groom. Their "Woody" or "Hedgehog" mane and tail brushes fit into small hands and are easier than a handled brush to use without breaking your pony's hair. The goat-hair face brush is super soft and also just the size for small hands.

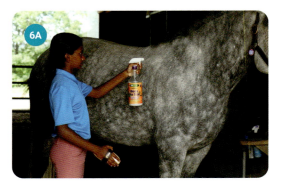

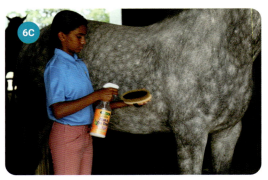

6 (A–C)

☆ **6 A–C** If your pony has a dry coat, you can use a *conditioner*. We like Equinature™ Aloe and Tea Tree. Hold the bottle several inches away and spray directly onto your horse **(A)**. Just a little goes a long way, so just one spritz, then move to a different area. Smooth the hair down with a towel, fuzzy mitt, or soft brush **(B)**.

THE KID'S GUIDE TO HORSEMANSHIP AND GROOMING / Cat Hill & Emma Ford

For the head, spray the conditioner onto the brush or towel **(C)**, then brush his face.

Mane and Tail Comb

☆ **7 A–G** Starting by the poll, comb your pony's mane over to one side **(A)**. If your pony has a wild mane and it doesn't want to lie down flat, apply some water to the mane and comb through again. You must take time with the tail. Ideally, you should apply a detangler product, such as Shapley's™ Magic Sheen, at the start of your grooming session and allow it to dry. Use a comb because a brush can break the hair. Start at the bottom of the tail and comb out a small section **(B)**. Move up the section only when the comb slides freely through the hair **(C)**. If you yank, it breaks the hair and can hurt the

7 (A–G)

CHAPTER 3 / Daily Grooming

41

8 (A–K)

THE KID'S GUIDE TO HORSEMANSHIP AND GROOMING / Cat Hill & Emma Ford

42

horse. Work your way all the way up the section, then add more hair in until you can comb through the entire tail. You should have three small sponges labeled "E" for eyes, "N" for nose, and "D" for dock **(D)**. Dampen each of your sponges and gently wipe away built-up dirt from the eyes **(E)**, nose **(F)**, and dock **(G)**. The sponges should all be rinsed after every use and only used on their specific area.

Hoof Pick

☆ **8 A–K** Checking your pony's feet is always number one on the grooming routine. Make sure there are no stones, sticks, or other debris in the foot that could be harmful. Starting with the left front leg, stand facing your pony's tail, close to the leg **(A)**. With the hoof pick in your right hand, run your left hand down the back of the pony's leg, starting from his elbow toward his heels **(B)**. Never go straight to the hoof as this can startle your pony. As you get to the fetlock, squeeze the leg slightly to indicate that you would like your pony to pick up his foot **(C)**. When the horse lifts his foot, slide your hand around the hoof to hold the coronet band **(D)**. With the hoof in your left hand, take the hoof pick in your right, and starting from the top of the foot, scrape downward toward the toe **(E)**. Use enough pressure to loosen the dirt out of the bottom of the hoof **(F)**. The *frog* makes a "V" in the middle of the hoof. It is sensitive tissue and only light pressure should be used to clean dirt away from the cracks and crevasses. Move on to the back left. Start with lightly patting your pony on his hindquarters to let him know where you are standing **(G)**. Position yourself close to the hind leg and run your hand down the side of it **(H)**. As with the front leg, squeeze when approaching the fetlock area to ask your pony to pick up his foot **(I)**. Once he lifts his foot, your hand should be supporting the hoof from the inside **(J)**. This is for safety. If your horse decides to take his leg away, he will go backward, and your arm will not be taken with it, preventing it from getting twisted or possibly dislocated. Pick out the foot in the same manner as the front foot **(K)**. Move around to the right side and repeat the routine with both front and hind feet. This time you will hold each leg with your right hand and pick out the feet with your left hand.

PRO TIP
Do the Essentials Every Day

Not all of us have endless time at the barn. If you only have a short window for grooming, like after school before homework, make sure to do the absolute essentials every day. It's easy to want to just use a quick stiff brush, because our ponies look the cleanest, but all that does is clean the top of the coat. Instead, if you are in a time crunch, make sure you curry, which brings up the deep dirt and gets air to the skin, preventing fungus.

Dust off the saddle area after you curry and pick the feet. While we encourage taking the time to do a proper groom whenever you can, this will at least help to make sure your pony's skin stays healthy. Take time on other days to do a deep groom.

Hoof Oil

The final step! If possible, do this outside on a hard surface where shavings, straw, and sand won't automatically stick to the hoof. Hoof oil helps to prevent the hoof from drying out or getting waterlogged.

☆ **9 A–C** Apply oil to the underside of the hoof, sole, and frog area **(A & B)**. Then apply to the outer wall, coronet band down **(C)**. Now you have a clean, shiny pony!

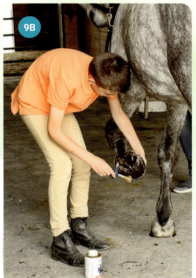

9 (A–C)

THE KID'S GUIDE TO HORSEMANSHIP AND GROOMING / Cat Hill & Emma Ford

44

Safety First!

Your own safety must always come first when working around your pony. Having an adult in the area is a good idea, especially if your pony has areas that he can get grumpy about when you try and clean them. When grooming, always put yourself in a position so you can move away easily and quickly should your pony have a "bad manners day."

☆ **11** While moving around him, do not duck under his head; if he bites at a fly on his chest or just bobs his head, you can get knocked down. If he picks up a front foot you can get bumped and stepped on. Instead, go around and under the cross-ties, not his head.

☆ **12 A & B** Never put your knees on the ground. If your horse moves, you are in danger of being stepped on or kicked **(A)**. Instead, crouch with

12 (A & B)

CHAPTER 3 / Daily Grooming

45

13 (A & B)

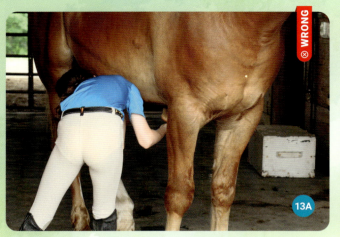
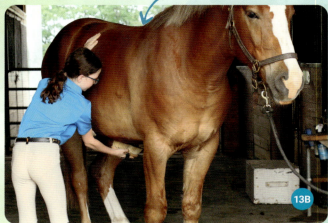

your feet under you so you can move quickly out of the way **(B)**.

☆ **13 A & B** Never put your head under your horse's body when grooming him; it is too easy to be kicked **(A)**. Instead, reach your arm under with your head up **(B)**.

☆ **14 A & B** If your pony gets too close to the wall, use pressure on his side and say, "Over," to ask him to give you some space **(A)**. If he swings his hips toward you, put one hand on his rear and one on his flank and ask him to move just his rear end over **(B)**.

☆ **15** When you are in a busy barn, take care when walking horses past each other. A horse on the cross-ties should have one side dropped and his handler standing next to his head. In the picture, you can see that Beau has his hips toward the wall, and his head and shoulders a little bit

14 (A & B)

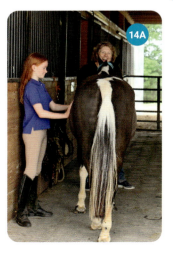

THE KID'S GUIDE TO HORSEMANSHIP AND GROOMING / Cat Hill & Emma Ford

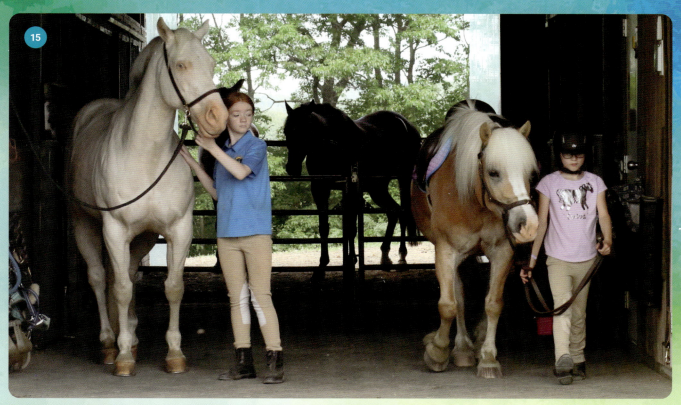

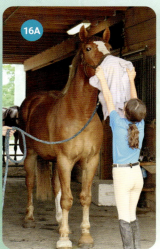
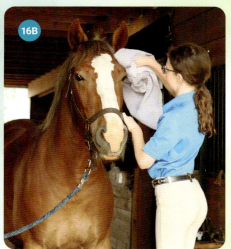

16 (A & B)

away. This helps prevent him from cow kicking or swinging his hind end toward the other pony. Milka, who is walking out of the barn, is positioned far enough from the wall to not get any tack caught, but far enough from Beau to give him space. Both leaders have their eyes up and are paying attention.

Grooming the Head

☆**16 A & B** If your pony likes to lift his head when you go to brush or towel it off, try standing on a mounting block on either side of his head **(A & B)**. Remember, ponies have a blind spot in the middle of their foreheads, so

CHAPTER 3 / *Daily Grooming*

18 (A–E)

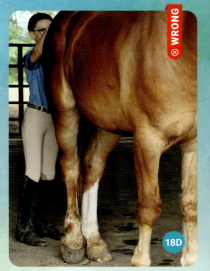

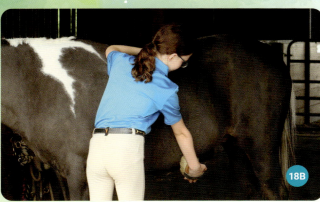
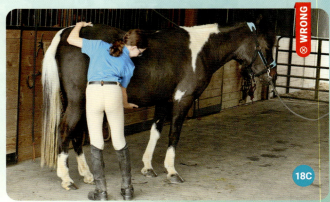

any quick movement will catch them off guard. Ponies are more comfortable when your arms are at their eye level rather than reaching over their eyes. This goes for bathing faces as well.

☆ **17** Talk to your pony and put a light hold on the halter as you brush or sponge his head. This way, if he moves, you have better control over your own balance.

The Kicking and Biting Zone

Common sensitive spots to groom can be the stomach, sheath/udder area, and between the

THE KID'S GUIDE TO HORSEMANSHIP AND GROOMING / Cat Hill & Emma Ford

48

back legs. Always talk to your pony and place your free hand on your pony's shoulder or rump to let him know you're going to touch him.

☆**18 A–E** Pay close attention to you pony's ears as you brush him. A flick of the ears, a swish of the tail, or a raised leg tells you your pony is uncomfortable being touched in an area **(A)**. As you move toward the sheath/udder, face your pony's tail and stay close to his side **(B)**. If you stand next to his leg and he kicks out, you are in range to be injured **(C)**. NEVER stand directly behind the pony **(D)**. Always stand a little to the side when working on the tail **(E)**. A straight-back kick is very forceful and can fling you to the floor or into a wall very easily.

Appropriate Attire

☆**19 A–C** It is important to outfit yourself safely in the barn. Long hair should be tied back neatly so it doesn't get caught in anything or get in your face **(A)**. Closed-toe shoes or boots should be worn **(B)**. Crocs, sneakers, and other soft-closed toes do not do a good job of protecting your toes from injury and should *not* be worn **(C)**.

19 (A–C)

end of chapter 3

CHAPTER 3 / Daily Grooming

49

chapter four

Getting Ready to Ride—Tacking Up

Getting Ready to Ride—Tacking Up

Your pony is clean and now it is time to tack up and ride! So, what equipment do you need?

☆**1** To be efficient get all your equipment together before you start to tack up.

- Saddle
- Saddle Pad
- Half Pad (Optional)
- Girth
- Breast Plate (Optional)
- Martingale (Optional)
- Bridle

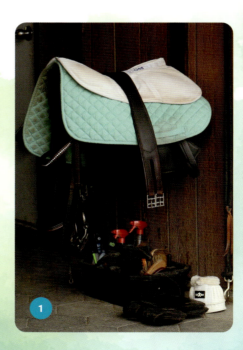

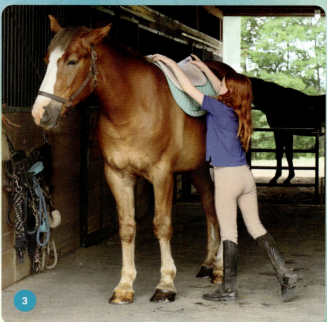

Saddle Up

Saddle Pad

☆2 Take the saddle pad and put it over your pony's withers. You never want to pull the pony's coat in the wrong direction, so always place the pad a little too far forward and then slide back into position. It should cover the withers and end before the last rib you can feel by the flank.

Half Pad (Optional)

☆3 The half pad should be placed on top of the saddle pad. The edges should match up with the saddle pad.

Saddle

☆4 A–E (next page) If your own height makes it difficult to put on the saddle then find a step stool to make this process easier (A). Standing on the near side, hold the saddle at the pommel and cantle (B). Lift the saddle over your horse's back, doing your best to lift it high enough to clear his back, rather than drag it over (C). Place the saddle lightly on the back (D). With your left hand, pick up the saddle pad in front of the pommel and lift it into the gullet; with your right hand, do the same at the cantle end. This prevents the pad from rubbing this area, which can be very sensitive (E). Now, step back and make sure the saddle is sitting in

CHAPTER 4 / Getting Ready to Ride—Tacking Up

53

4 (A–E)

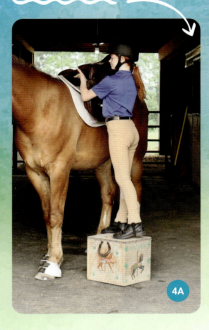

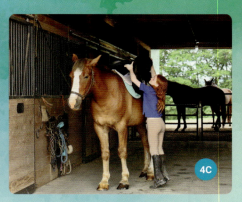
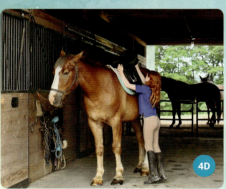

the correct spot. If it is too far *forward*, just slide the pad and saddle back into position. If too far *back,* you need to lift the saddle pad and saddle simultaneously off the horse's back and place farther forward, again making sure you then slide the saddle into place going *with* the direction of hair growth, not against it.

Girth

☆**5 A–E** The girth should be attached first, from the off (right) side; the buckles should be at least two holes from the bottom, *not* on the very top holes **(A)**. When you have three billets, you should do up to the first and third billet. This applies a more even pressure across the tree of the saddle. The third billet is a safety measure in case one of the other two breaks. Moving to the near (left) side, take the girth under the belly **(B)**. When you have a breastplate/martingale (see p. 56), put the girth through the loop before you buckle it **(C)**. Do the girth up just snugly enough to hold the saddle

PRO TIP
Make Sure the Girth Is Comfortable

Before mounting, pull your horse's legs forward to help stretch out any skin folds under the girth that might cause chafing. Stand to the side of the horse, a little in front of his leg and run your hand down one leg toward the knee (A). Lift the knee up and forward, being careful not to fight the horse; just a gentle stretch will do the trick (B). Gently set the leg down and do the other side.

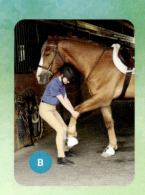

5 (A–E)

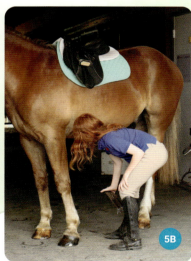

CHAPTER 4 / Getting Ready to Ride—Tacking Up

55

in place **(D)**. Don't over-tighten. This is uncomfortable for your pony. Do not do the last tightening until you have walked your pony a few steps forward. The girth should sit about a hand's width away from your pony's elbow **(E)**.

Breastplate or Martingale (Optional)

Note that if you use one, a breastplate and martingale should be put around the pony's neck *before* you put on the saddle. If you have the option, I like to undo the collar and rebuckle it around the pony's neck. This way you do not need to untie the pony. In addition, if he is a little head shy, it is a more compassionate way to put on the tack. Next, place your saddle pad and saddle as we've already described.

☆**6 A–G** Attach the right side of the girth first, then walk around to the left side of the horse and, reaching under him, grab the breastplate loop and the girth **(A)**. Slide the girth through the breastplate loop, making sure there aren't any twists in either one **(B)**. Buckle the left side of the girth to the billets **(C)**. Attach the top straps of the breastplate to the

6 (A–C)

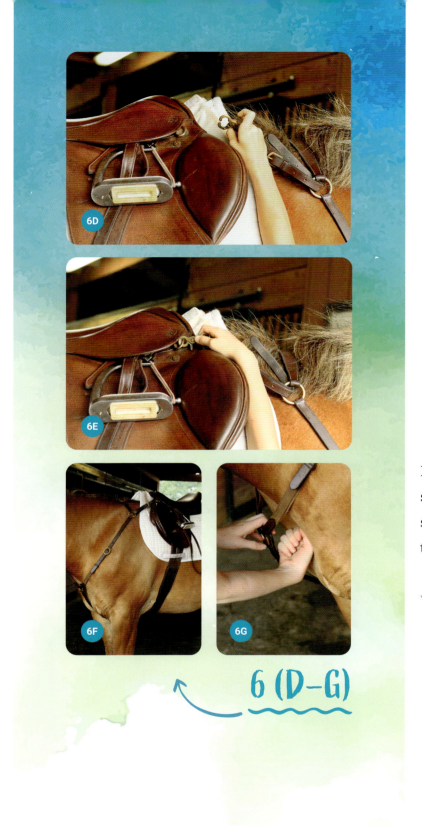

6 (D–G)

saddle dee rings **(D & E)**. Never do the top straps of a breastplate or martingale before the girth is attached; if the pony moves and the saddle is connected to the breastplate but not the girth, it can slide off then hang under the horse, causing a scare. The breastplate should rest with the top piece just in front of the withers, and the girth strap in the center of the horse's chest. There should be a fist's-width between the horse's chest and the center ring **(F & G)**.

Bridle

First, have your bridle over your left shoulder and make sure the reins are sitting on top of the head piece and not twisted.

☆**7 A–R (next page)** Unbuckle the top strap of the halter **(A)**. Keep holding the top strap and the buckle and lower the halter down the horse's nose. Once off his nose, buckle the halter back up around his neck **(B)**. You always want to have something around your horse's neck so you can hold onto him if he likes to wander off! Now place the reins over the horse's head onto the neck **(C)**. Hold the crownpiece of the bridle and use

PRO TIP
Get a Step Up

If your pony's height is an issue, or he likes to put his head up when you put the bridle on, use a step stool.

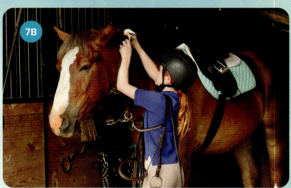

7 (A–C)

your left hand to hold the bit flat, palm open. Place the bit to your horse's lips, and for added encouragement, put the thumb of your left hand in the corner of your pony's mouth **(D)**. A well-trained pony will open his mouth allowing you to slide the bit in at the same time as your right hand pulls the headpiece up and over the ears **(E)**. When your pony has a bridle path, make sure the mane separates correctly under the headpiece, and gently pull his ears forward and pull the forelock out over the browband **(F & G)**. Buckle the throatlatch first **(H)**. The throatlatch should be no tighter than a flat hand **(I)**. Then check that both sides of the noseband are under the cheekpieces **(J)**. The noseband should sit two fingers below the cheekbone. Make sure it is straight before doing it up—you should be able to easily fit two to three fingers between it and your pony's nose when buckled **(K)**. Check to see the bit is over

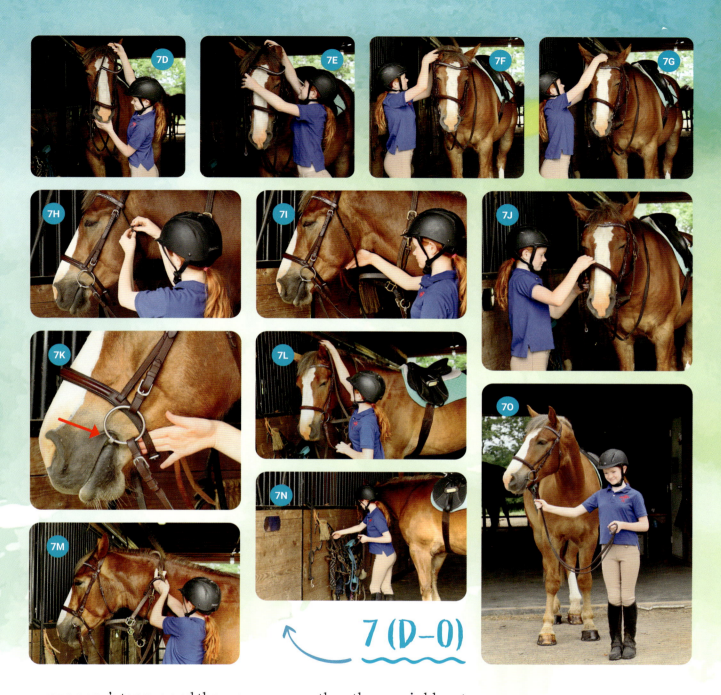

7 (D–O)

your pony's tongue and there are no more than three wrinkles at the corner of your pony's mouth (see red arrow 7K). Now bring the reins up and over the ears **(L)**. Unclick the halter from the cross-ties and take the halter from around his neck **(M)**. Hang up the halter where it cannot get stepped on or tangled in **(N)**. Now you are ready to ride! **(O)**

CHAPTER 4 / Getting Ready to Ride—Tacking Up

59

chapter five

Leg Care and Protection

Leg Care and Protection

Take a step back and look at the shape of your horse. You can see that his legs are very thin when compared to his body. In fact, most horses' legs are smaller around at the cannon bone than most adult humans' legs! Because of this, horses' legs are prone to injury and problems.

Horses' legs can get hurt when you ride them hard or jump lots of jumps. You need to check them after a tough workout.

Feeling for Leg Issues

There are special ways of caring for and protecting legs to prevent injury. How do you tell when the legs are hurt or sore in some way?

First, you must know what the legs feel like normally. To do this, you teach your hands to feel for problems. Here are a couple exercises—note that the pads of your fingers can only feel when you don't push hard.

☆**1 A–E** Take your hands and put them palm-down on a table in front of you, then watch your fingernails closely, and slowly

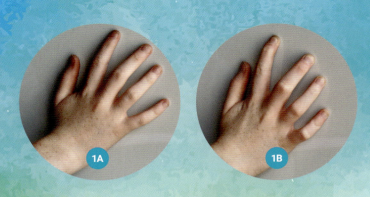

push down **(A)**. As soon as your fingernails change color, you are pushing too hard to feel problems on a horse's leg **(B)**. Next, find a small pebble or a dried bean. Put this pebble under a piece of paper, then run your hand over the paper, being careful not to squish so hard you change your fingernail color **(C & D)**. Can you feel the pebble? That's great! Now, take another paper and add it. Can you still feel the pebble? Keep adding paper until you have a hard time finding the pebble with your fingertips **(E)**. Then practice until you can locate the pebble!

Protective Boots

Brushing Boots

Sometimes, you need to use boots to help prevent your pony from hurting himself. When you regularly ride your pony and on your return to the barn you see marks on his inside fetlocks, he may need *brushing boots*. These will prevent him from hurting himself when he taps one of his fetlocks with his opposite foot.

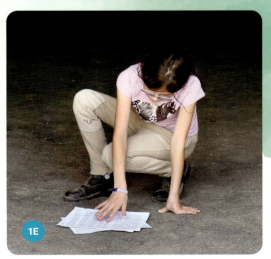

1 (A–E)

CHAPTER 5 / *Leg Care and Protection*

63

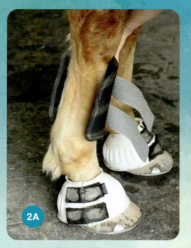
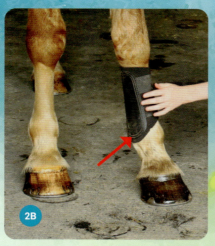

2 (A–E)

Brushing boots are very common and come in many different sizes, materials, fastenings, and colors. These boots protect the inside of the leg from below the knee to just below the fetlock. Most of the padding should be seen on the inside of the leg. To put on correctly, the straps must always go on the outside with the end toward the horse's tail.

☆ **2 A–E** Place the boot slightly above the knee and push down into position so the hair is always going in the correct direction **(A)**. The bottom of the boot should cover the inside of the fetlock but not be touching the pastern **(B)**. When the boot has *two straps*, do up the bottom one first **(C)**, then the second strap **(D)**. For boots with *three straps*, do the middle, then the bottom, and then the top. The outside of the boots should sit just below the knee and end just above the fetlock **(E)**. When

THE KID'S GUIDE TO HORSEMANSHIP AND GROOMING / *Cat Hill & Emma Ford*

3 (A–H)

you push down on them, they should not slide down. If they do, undo them, and start again.

☆ **3 A–H** Boots with *double lock straps* can be a bit tricky. Imagine that the extra strap, usually the "hook" of the Velcro, isn't there. The front of the boot has the "loop" part of the Velcro. This one should be coming from the inside of the leg to the outside, with the ends toward the horse's tail **(A)**. Do the bottom strap first **(B)**. Now apply the extra bottom strap **(C & D)**. Next, pull the top strap snug and attach it **(E)**. Finally apply the extra strap over the first **(F & G)**. The second set of straps is there to stop the boots from coming undone. When done up correctly, these boots may look as if you have them on backward **(H)**, but it's the direction of the *first* set of straps that matter!

Bell Boots

Over-reaching, commonly known as *forging,* means a horse steps on the back of his front feet with his hind feet. You might hear "clicking" when your pony catches his front shoes. To protect against him hurting himself, you will need a

CHAPTER 5 / Leg Care and Protection

65

PRO TIP
Boots for Turnout

If your pony requires bell boots for turnout, do not use fleece-collared bell boots because they can cause the horse to sweat and will absorb moisture from the dew or rain and remain wet for long periods of time—not allowing the back of the pastern to dry and breathe. Always take the bell boots off when your pony comes in to his stall or for grooming in order to prevent irritation.

4 (A–C)

pair of *bell boots*. These sit around the pastern and over the bulbs of the heel. As with brushing boots, there are many varieties but the easiest ones to use have Velcro fasteners.

☆ **4 A–G** Start by putting them around the pastern **(A)**. Bell boots should be able to spin freely around the leg, so put these on with the topmost Velcro facing *away* from the inside of the hoof. So with a double-lock Velcro, point the first set of Velcro to the inside **(B)**. The final strap gets smoothed over, facing the outside of the hoof **(C)**. When you put them on, make sure there is a finger's width between the pastern and boot. This helps prevent the boot from rubbing the back of the pastern and causing irritation. Never stand directly in front of the knee when positioning any boot **(D)**. This bell boot is upside down **(E)**.

4 (D–G)

Always let your pony know where you are about to work with a gentle stroke on his shoulder or hindquarters, followed by running your hand down his leg **(F & G)**.

Post-Work Leg Care

In addition to being protected from getting banged on, your horse's legs need to be cared for after they have had a really hard workout. It's important to think about a few things when you decide what is "hard" for your horse. If he isn't used to doing work outside, a trail ride can be hard work, even if it's only at the walk, because of the change in ground and the hills. When he is older, jumping, cantering, and big hills can make him sore. If he hasn't been in regular work, several days in a row of work can make the third day of work seem like more than it would otherwise. Every time you put a horse in the trailer, that's a workout. Standing in a moving vehicle is difficult and tiring for even a quiet, well-traveled horse.

A horse's legs can show the strain of a workout more than other places, so it's a good idea to spend a little extra time caring for them.

Liniment

Liniment is a great way to help the blood keep circulating to the legs, which helps the horse feel better faster. Arnica-based liniments are less likely to cause a tingle or burning sensation so are our first choice. We like Equinature™ LegDown™. Witch hazel also is a great choice for leg care. Putting the liniment in a spray bottle will help you get the whole leg covered without wasting it from spillage onto the ground.

CHAPTER 5 / Leg Care and Protection

67

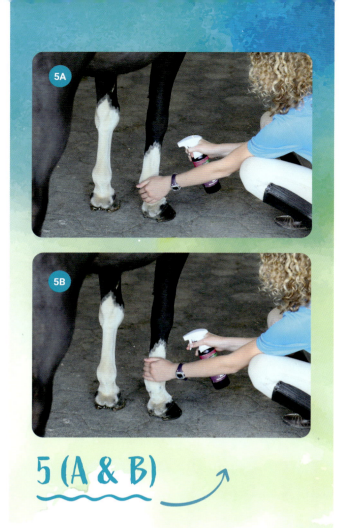

5 (A & B)

☆ **5 A & B** Spray the leg all over **(A)**. Use your hands to rub the liniment into your horse's skin **(B)**.

Leg Wraps

We use leg wraps for horses who are riding in a trailer or who need some extra care for their lower limbs. Wrapping a horse's legs is a good option if your horse is staying inside but can be very dangerous when done incorrectly. Due to the difficulty in doing a standing wrap correctly, we prefer to start with an all-in-one wrap. Rambo® Ionic leg wraps are our favorites, but there are several good ones on the market. Look for a breathable neoprene shell and

6 (A–D)

a pillow wrap that attaches to the inside of the boot.

☆ **6 A–I** To put on an all-in-one wrap, first place the wrap around the leg so the straps can be pulled across the front and to the outside **(A)**. Slide the boot into place so the boot "cups" the fetlock **(B)**. Take the middle strap across the

THE KID'S GUIDE TO HORSEMANSHIP AND GROOMING / Cat Hill & Emma Ford

PRO TIP
Keep a Horse Care Diary

Use a notebook as a "Horse Care Diary," and keep track of your pony's health and training. As you get to know your pony's legs, write down any time the legs have little cuts, swellings, or other issues. Some horses get "thick" lower legs when they have been standing in a stall for a long time (called stocking-up). It's good to keep track of when this happens so you don't get worried about it when you go to a horse show and see it happen after your pony has stood in a stall all day.

front of the leg and then around the back of the boot so it is securely fastened **(C & D)**. Take the bottom strap and cup the fetlock by first lowering the strap down and around the pastern, then come back up to fasten across the front of the fetlock **(E–G)**. Now take the top strap and secure across the front and to the outside of the leg as you did with the middle strap **(H & I)**.

end of chapter 5

6 (E–I)

CHAPTER 5 / Leg Care and Protection

69

chapter six

Post-Workout Bathing

Post-Workout Bathing

Bathing your horse after a workout seems like it should be nice for him, but often, our horses don't agree with us! Here are some tips to help make this important task less stressful.

There is a difference between *bathing* and *rinsing*. When we say *bathing*, it means using soap to help get the horse clean. *Rinsing* means getting a horse wet only, and we normally use this to help him cool off.

There are two options available to you when bathing your pony, depending on what setup you have available—bathing *with* a wash rack or *without* one. But before we get to that, let's talk about a simple post-work rinse.

Bucket Rinsing

☆**1 A–L** *Bucket rinsing* is useful when you are cooling your horse off after a ride and do not have a hose or are out on an adventure at a showground **(A)**. When the weather is hot, try to find a shady spot with a breeze **(B)**. Here, Ivy is having her bucket rinse to help her cool down under the shade of a tree. Make sure you start at the shoulder, not the face. Coming at a horse's

1 (A–H)

face with a dripping sponge can be scary! Stand next to the shoulder, with your bucket a little bit away from you and your horse, so if he moves, he doesn't step in it. Fill the sponge with water, don't squeeze it out, then put it on the horse, pressing it so the water squishes out and down his body **(C)**. Repeat this as you move toward the rear of the horse **(D)**. Wet the horse's sides, legs, and neck. Do not forget under the tail and between the legs **(E)**. Now, take your sponge, dunk

CHAPTER 6 / Post-Workout Bathing

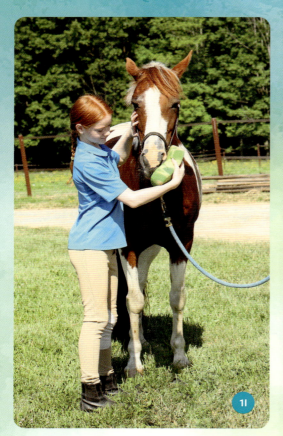

1 (I–L)

it in the water, and squeeze it out so only a little water is still in it **(F)**. Stand next to and just behind your horse's head **(G)**. Rub the sponge on the horse's cheek, then up over the center of the face and down the front of the head **(H–I)**. Repeat on the other side. If you are simply cooling a horse out or rinsing the sweat off, you can scrape off the excess water with a sweat-scraper **(J & K)**. Next use a towel to dry off the legs and face. Letting Ivy have a pick of grass while drying in the shade makes for a happy horse **(L)**.

Bathing with a Wash Rack

For special events, you will want to do a full "scrubbly-bubbly" bath. With a wash rack available, follow the instructions coming up next. If not, skip to the section called Bathing without Wash Rack (p. 82).

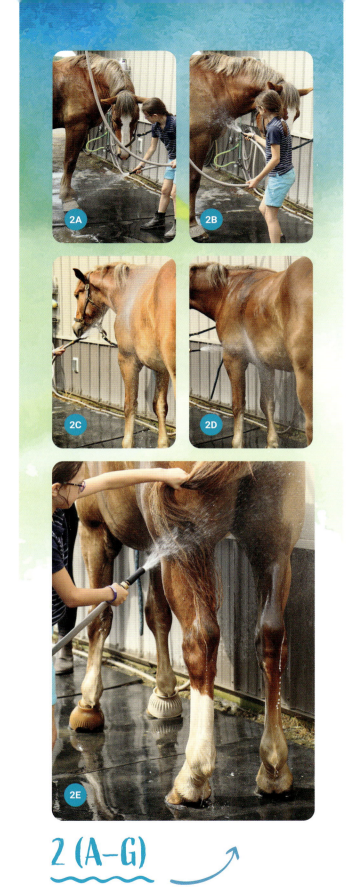

2 (A–G)

Wetting Down

⭐ **2 A–G** Once your horse is on the wash rack, turn on the hose and start by spraying the ground a little in front of the horse's front feet **(A)**. Phineas is young, so he looks at the water, but he doesn't seem concerned or worried, so Adelaide slowly keeps going. Work your way up his leg toward his shoulder **(B)**, then along his back to get your entire horse wet **(C)**. Make sure you get the girth area and between the front legs **(D)**. Hold the tail out of the way as you do between his back legs **(E)**. Looking at the photos of Ivy, you can see how important rinsing is! She looked clean prior to wetting her down, but on Ivy's back you can see the line of dirt on her pink skin. The top area is nice and pink

CHAPTER 6 / Post-Workout Bathing

75

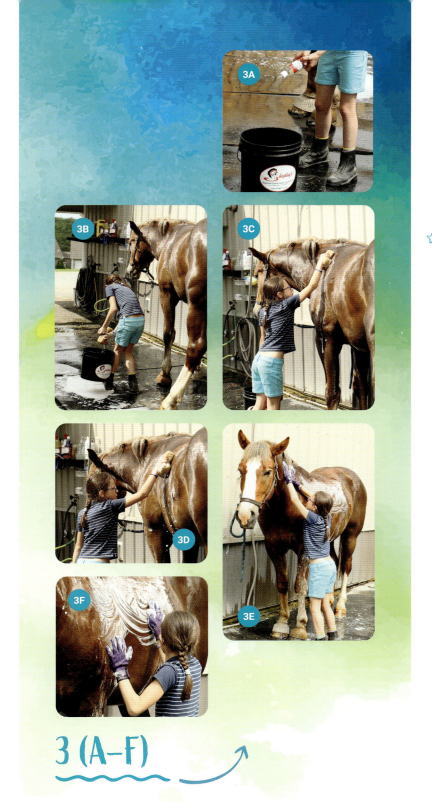

3 (A–F)

while the bottom is dark because it still has dirt **(F)**. The line moves down her white spot as the water "chases" the dirt down her back **(G)**.

Soaping

☆**3 A–F** Once your horse is all wet, get a bucket and fill it with several inches of water, making sure it's easy to lift. Then pour some shampoo into the bucket, just enough to make some good bubbles **(A)**. Use a shampoo specifically made for horses, since they are meant to be diluted and still work. Take your bucket in one hand, the sponge in your other, and walk over to your horse. Starting at the shoulder, take the sponge from the bucket, put it onto the horse, and start scrubbing **(B & C)**. Cover the entire horse this way, from his ears to his tail, getting him nice and bubbly **(D)**. Now, grab a good curry comb and scrub, working the soap deep into his coat, all over his body. Scrub his legs and the rest of him **(E & F)**.

Mane

Phineas has a flaxen mane and tail, which has light blond and silver streaks in it. So, we will use a purple

THE KID'S GUIDE TO HORSEMANSHIP AND GROOMING / *Cat Hill & Emma Ford*

whitening shampoo on these areas. If his mane and tail were dark, we would use the same shampoo as we used on his body.

☆ **4 A & B** For his mane, pour the shampoo straight into your hand **(A)**. Work the shampoo into his mane and scrub with your fingers deep into the crest **(B)**.

Tail

☆ **5 A & B** For the tail, stand to the side of the hindquarters, put shampoo directly on your hand, and work it into the dock with your fingers and all the way down his tail **(A & B)**.

CHAPTER 6 / Post-Workout Bathing

  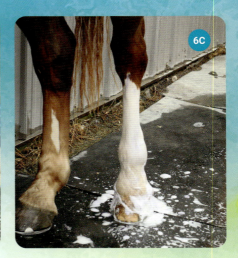

6 (A–C)

Socks

Phineas also has a white sock, so we will use the purple shampoo there as well.

☆ **6 A–C** Put the shampoo right in your hand and first smooth it over the white sock **(A)**. Then rub up and down and use your fingertips to get deep into the hair until the shampoo turns from purple to white **(B)**. Make sure the entire sock is covered in bright white bubbles, then let the shampoo sit on for 10 to 15 minutes before rinsing it off **(C)**.

Face

Use a sponge to do his face. First get it wet, then squeeze it out so it's barely dripping.

☆ **7 A–D** Rub the damp sponge all over his face, standing at the side **(A)**. Then use a tiny amount of shampoo on your sponge or in your hands and gently scrub his face **(B)**. Finally, rinse off with a damp sponge again **(C)**. Note: it's important *not* to stand directly in front of the horse while you wash him **(D)**. In this picture, Adelaide is in danger! If Phineas were to toss his

7 (A–D)

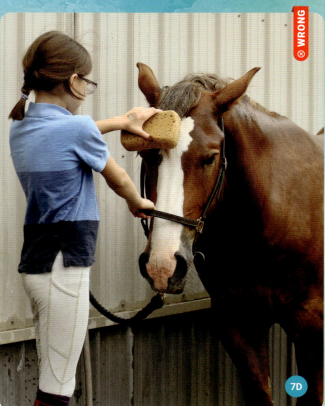

head, he would hit her in the chin and knock her off the stool. Standing at the side is always a better option.

Rinsing

✩ **8 A–F** Once you've finished washing the horse's face, grab the hose for the rinse. Start the hose on the ground, work up a front leg to his shoulder, and then back toward his tail **(A & B)**. Make sure you use plenty of water and rinse until the water runs clear **(C)**. Once he's all rinsed, it's time to use a sweat-scraper to squeeze off the excess water. Starting at the neck, grasp the scraper in two hands and pull the scraper along his coat, pushing the water out of his hair **(D–F)**.

8 (A)

CHAPTER 6 / Post-Workout Bathing

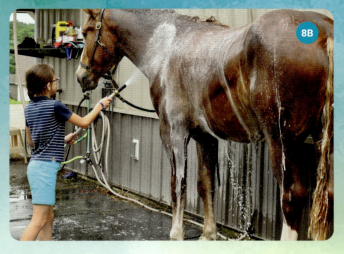

Drying

☆**9 A–E** Once the horse has been scraped, get a dry towel. Using two hands, grasp the towel, wrap it around each leg, and rub it down the whole leg **(A & B)**. Towel off his face. Stand a little to the side (a stool can be useful here!) and show him the towel to sniff **(C)**. If you push the towel at him abruptly, he may pull away. **(D)** Instead, give him a second to relax, then rub the towel across his face, especially the hollows above his eyes and the bony bits on the side of his face **(E)**.

THE KID'S GUIDE TO HORSEMANSHIP AND GROOMING / Cat Hill & Emma Ford

9 (C–E)

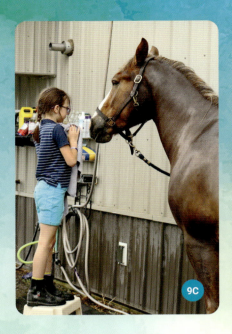

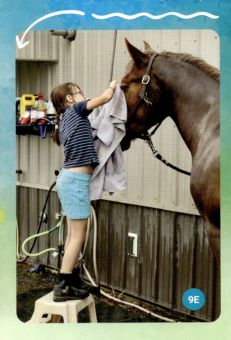

Mane and Tail Care

⭐ **10 A & B** Once your horse is toweled off, comb his mane down smoothly, which will help prevent crazy hair after the bath. Use a detangler on his tail **(A)**. We use Shapley's Magic Sheen. Hold the tail to the side and spray from 6 to 8 inches away **(B)**. Spray the whole tail thoroughly; in this instance, a little more is better. It will help his tail be easy to comb and look nice for a couple days. Make sure you let the tail dry completely before you comb it, as wet hair breaks easily.

10 (A & B)

CHAPTER 6 / Post-Workout Bathing

81

11 (A–G)

Bathing without a Wash Rack

Wetting Down

When you do *not* have a wash rack, you bathe kind of like you give a bucket rinse. Find a dry spot of grass to stand your pony on. Dirt turns to mud, so grass is a better option. Have a friend or parent hold your pony so you can wash him thoroughly, and have a few buckets of clean water nearby.

☆ **11 A–G** Dip your sponge completely in the water and lift it out **(A)**. Don't squeeze it! Now, carry the sponge to your pony, and starting at the neck, squeeze the sponge out on the pony to get

THE KID'S GUIDE TO HORSEMANSHIP AND GROOMING / Cat Hill & Emma Ford

him wet. You can see the water running down Ivy's shoulder getting her nice and wet **(B)**. Get more water and repeat the "dunk and squeeze" all along the pony, from front to back **(C)**. Don't forget to do his legs, too. Start at the top of the leg and let the water run down **(D & E)**. Rinse between the back legs by holding the tail to the side and gently rubbing the sponge between them **(F)**. Do between the front legs, too, standing to the side, and keeping your head up and away as you rub between them **(G)**.

Head

☆ **12 A–D** Now take your sponge, dip it in the water and squeeze it out so it isn't dripping at all **(A)**. Approach your pony's face and put one hand on the nose while the other reaches up and rubs the sponge on his forehead **(B)**. Run the sponge down his face and make sure to do his muzzle, mouth, and nostril area **(C & D)**.

Tail

☆ **13 A–C** To wet the tail, fill a bucket with water as far as you can and still lift it without struggling. Walk to the

12 (A–D)

CHAPTER 6 / *Post-Workout Bathing*

side of the horse's hind end, gather the tail up in one hand and dunk the entire base of the tail in the bucket **(A & B)**. Then take the sponge out of the bucket and squeeze it on the top of the tail **(C)**.

Soaping

☆**14 A–H** Now that Ivy is all wet, let's start soaping her up! Fill your bucket about halfway with water then pour the shampoo into the bucket. Remember, horse shampoo is strong; you don't need a lot, just a small amount. I like to count to three as I pour, which is a good amount. **(A)** Put your sponge in the water and stir it around, getting the shampoo mixed into the water. Then, starting at the neck and working your way back, rub your soapy sponge onto the horse **(B)**. For the mane and tail, put a little shampoo directly on your hands and rub them together until you get a nice lather **(C)**. Now, work your hands into your horse's crest, using your fingers to give a good scrub **(D)**. Do the same for the top of the tail **(E)** and work your way down the dock **(F & G)**. Flatten out your hands and rub the hair between them **(H)**. Once you have soaped up the entire pony, repeat the steps you used for wetting down, now using the water to rinse out all the soap from his coat, mane, and tail. Make sure you get the *whole pony* rinsed with lots of clean water. Leaving soap on him anywhere will irritate his skin.

13 (A–C)

THE KID'S GUIDE TO HORSEMANSHIP AND GROOMING / *Cat Hill & Emma Ford*

84

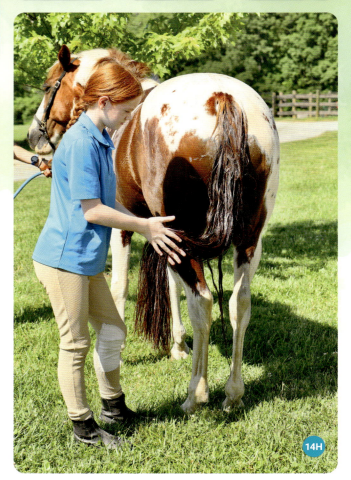

14 (A–H)

Light-Colored Horses

When you have a horse that is white, gray, or pinto, you have a couple of options. First, bathe him following the instructions on page either page 74 or 82. Whitening shampoos cannot do their job when there is dirt still in the hair. The key to bright white hair is: clean first, then whiten! After you have washed him, you will need a whitening shampoo. We love Shapley's™ Equitone for light horses.

CHAPTER 6 / Post-Workout Bathing

15 (A & B)

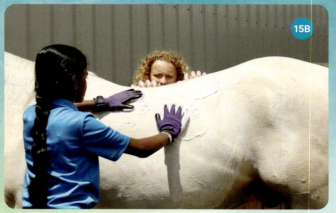

☆ **15 A & B** Pour the shampoo right onto your horse. Using HandsOn® gloves will help get down to the skin, but if you don't have them, just scrub with your bare hands **(A)**. Rub until the purple shampoo turns into white bubbles **(B)**. Now move on to a different spot and repeat the process.

Legs

16 (A–C)

☆ **16 A–C** For his legs, pour the shampoo in your hands **(A)**. Smooth it down the leg, paying special attention to hocks and knees, which collect stains **(B)**. Rub the shampoo in with your fingertips until the purple shampoo disappears into white bubbles **(C)**.

THE KID'S GUIDE TO HORSEMANSHIP AND GROOMING / Cat Hill & Emma Ford

Tail

☆ **17 A–C** Squirt the shampoo directly onto the tail, starting at the top and working your way down **(A)**. Rub the tail vigorously until the purple disappears into white bubbles **(B)**. You can sandwich the hair between your hands and rub back and forth to create lots of friction **(C)**. If you leave the purple shampoo on without scrubbing it into bubbles, you may accidentally turn your gray horse into a purple one! Once you have scrubbed enough for white bubbles, let the shampoo sit on the horse for 10 to 15 minutes, then rinse.

Rinsing

☆ **18 A–D (next page)** Remember to start at the bottom of the legs and work your way up as you rinse **(A & B)**. Rinse the tail until the water runs clear and has no bubbles in it **(C)**. It's a good idea to spray a silicone detangler and shine on the white areas if you are doing the bath the day before a show or special event. Be careful not to get any spray near the saddle area—it can be dangerous by causing your saddle to slip. Make sure the horse is dry before he goes into a stall. The shavings will make his legs dingy-looking again if they get on the wet hair. Beau shows off how he gleams in the sun after his bath **(D)**.

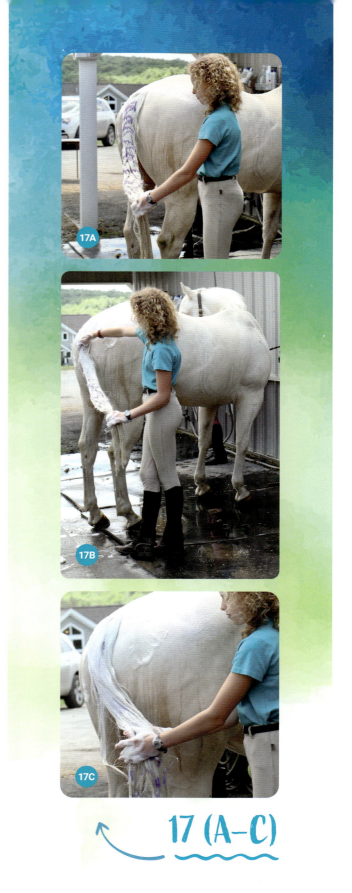

17 (A–C)

CHAPTER 6 / Post-Workout Bathing

87

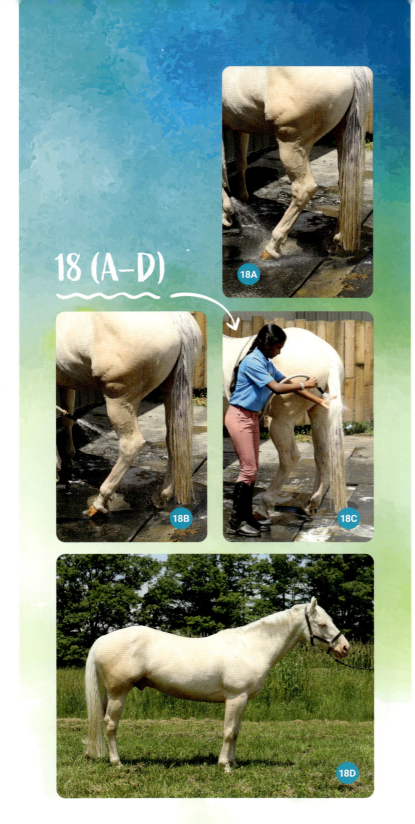

18 (A–D)

Cold or Below-Freezing Towel Bath

When it is cold out, or for some other reason you cannot bathe your horse, here are a couple options:

– *When chilly but not below freezing,* wash your horse's legs and tail and put an extra blanket on to keep him warm while he dries.

– *When below freezing,* do a towel bath. First, get a couple of gallons of warm water. If you do not have a hot water spigot, there are bucket heaters you can put in water that will heat it up in about 10 minutes.

☆ **19 A–E** Once you have your warm water, add five or six drops of Ivory® dish soap **(A)**. In this case, using a specific brand is important. You need a very gentle soap like Ivory because you will not be rinsing the soap off. Add a tablespoon of oil. Shapley's™ No. 1 Light Oil, baby oil, olive oil, or coconut oil all work well **(B)**. Stir the water, soap, and oil

19 (A–E)

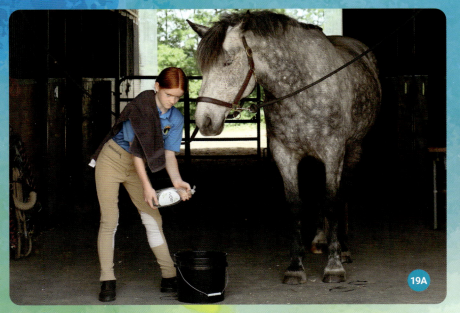
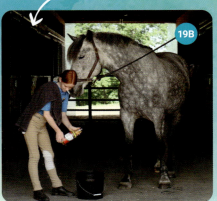

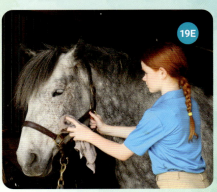

together really well. Then take a towel, put it completely in the water and squeeze it as hard as you can until no more water streams out **(C)**. Take your towel and rub it all over your horse, dunking it into the water mixture every few minutes **(D)**. Rub the cloth on his face and head as well **(E)**.

end of chapter 6

CHAPTER 6 / Post-Workout Bathing

chapter seven

Tack Cleaning

7

Tack Cleaning

Tack is very expensive. You need to take good care of the leather so it remains safe to use for a long time. You don't want a rein to break mid-canter! Every day you should make sure to wipe down your tack.

Bridle

Cleaning

☆**1 A–H** First, remove the bit and place it in a bucket of warm water **(A)**. Take a sponge or a small terrycloth towel and dunk it in some water, then wring it out **(B)**. Apply a little tack cleaner/conditioner to the rag. Then take the rag and scrub the leather vigorously, pulling the leather out of the keepers and getting all the dirt and sweat off **(C)**. Also do the reins **(D)**. Dry the bit off, wiping away any leftover bits of yuck **(E)**. Hang the bit back on the bridle and attach the reins **(F)**. When attaching the bit, be aware of how it hangs in your horse's mouth. Most bits have a *shaped mouthpiece*, which means it curves to make room for the horse's tongue. When you fold the bit in half one way, notice how it is shaped to create space for the tongue **(G)**. Turn it around and fold it the other way, and you can see how tight it is in the middle **(H)**. The shaped side should face the tongue side of the bridle.

Hanging the Bridle After Use

Once it's clean and back together, a clean bridle should be wrapped neatly to hang in the tack room. This not only looks nice but also has the purpose of keeping the leather in its correct shape.

☆**2 A–I (next page)** Hang the bridle over a hook. Take the throatlatch and bring it diagonally, downward around the front of the bridle **(A)**. As you pass it around the back of the bridle, make sure all the straps are collected inside the throatlatch **(B)**. Pass around to the front, this time diagonally upward and slide the throatlatch strap into the keepers, which helps prevent wear on the strap from the buckle **(C & D)**. Now pull the noseband out so the straps

1 (A–H)

CHAPTER 7 / Tack Cleaning

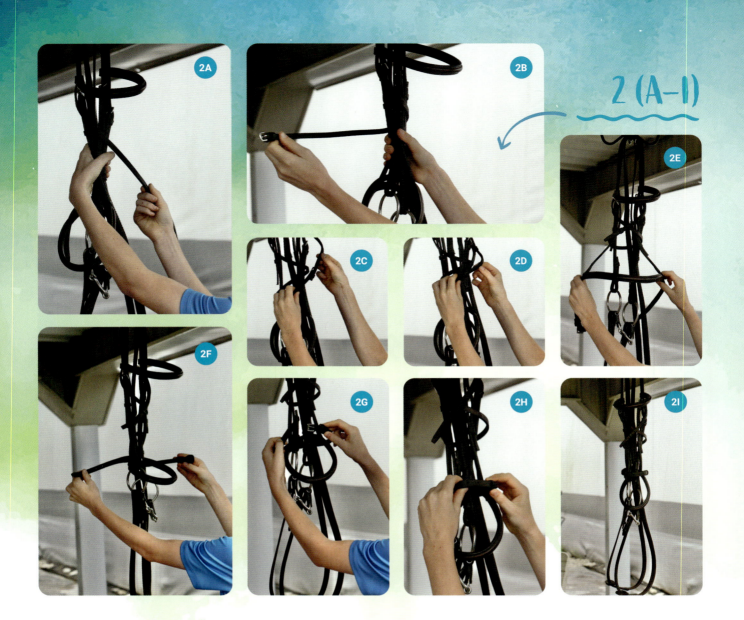

2 (A–I)

are outside the cheekpieces and reins **(E)**. Cross the noseband straps behind the cheekpieces and reins **(F)**. Back at the front of the bridle, insert the strap end into the keepers on the noseband **(G & H)**. Now the bridle is neatly ready to store **(I)**.

Taking Bridle Apart for Deep Cleaning

Periodically, you need to do a deep clean and condition your tack. You first need to learn how to take a bridle apart and put it back together.

☆ **3 A–E** Using a notepad and pen, write down the holes that are being used for the cheekpieces and noseband **(A)**. Then, undo all the buckles **(B & C)**. Some buckles can be stiff; you can use a hoof pick to lift the leather and get it undone. Put the hoof pick below the peg that holds the leather in place **(D)**. Once that is free, move the hoof pick to the other side and lift that side the same way **(E)**. Depending on the style of bridle, you should have at least eight separate pieces: the bit, two cheekpieces, one head piece, one noseband, the browband, and the reins. (Some bridles have detachable throat latches.)

Deep Cleaning

☆ **4 A–D (next page)** Once the bridle is taken apart, check all the folds in the leather for cracking, as well as all the stitching around the buckles **(A)**. Over time, stitching can rot, which is very unsafe.

CHAPTER 7 / Tack Cleaning

PRO TIP
Beat the Buildup

If there is a buildup of dirt and grease on the bridle leather, use the rough side of a dish sponge to remove it all. Then add a little leather soap, and the job will take no time at all.

4 (A–D)

It can be easily fixed by a leather repair shop, but you want to catch the signs early to prevent an accident. Place the bit in warm soapy water **(B)**. Use a damp rag to wipe over all the pieces of leather **(C)**. Make sure you move the keepers and get under and behind all the buckles **(D)**.

Conditioning Leather

☆ **5 A–C** Now you need to use conditioner. We like Tack Butter **(A)**. Using a separate sponge just for conditioner, rub it into the tack **(B)**, working it in very well where the leather attaches to the bit on the reins and cheekpieces **(C)**. How much conditioner you use depends on the dryness of

THE KID'S GUIDE TO HORSEMANSHIP AND GROOMING / Cat Hill & Emma Ford

5 (A–C)

PRO TIP
Deep Condition Twice a Year

At least twice a year, or when you get given some old—or brand new—tack, you need to deep condition the leather with Neatsfoot oil. Use the same process as described for conditioner, but now, allow the leather time to soak in all the oil.

Especially with new tack, you can help break it in by rolling the leather while applying the oil.

Make sure not to soak the tack overnight. Neatsfoot oil can break down the stitching when leather sits in it too long.

6 (A–I)

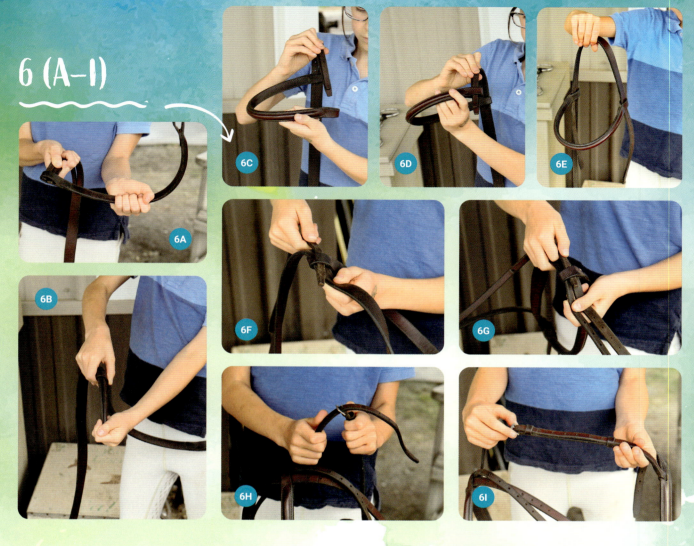

the leather. When there is excess that doesn't soak up, use a soft towel to wipe off the leather. You should be left with supple, not sticky tack.

Putting Bridle Back Together

Now that you have the bridle really clean, it's time to put it back together!

Crownpiece, Browband, and Noseband

☆ **6 A–I** Take the crownpiece and thread the browband through from the left side **(A)**. Pull the straps through the loop **(B)**, then down through the other side of the browband **(C & D)**. Check that this section is hanging correctly with no twists. Make sure the throatlatch is at the back of the browband **(E)**. Now thread the noseband underneath the headpiece and through the browband **(F & G)**. Buckle your noseband, remembering to check your notes for what hole it was on! **(H)** Tuck it into the keepers **(I)**.

Cheekpieces, Bit, and Reins

☆ **7 A–T** Next, it's time to add the cheekpieces. Make sure you hook the cheekpieces to the correct strap. The cheekpieces are thicker and should be toward the front of the browband **(A)**. Connect the cheekpieces to the crownpiece, checking your notes for the correct hole **(B)**. Tuck in the ends to the keepers **(C)**, and repeat for the other side **(D)**. Hang the bridle from the crownpiece on a hook and pick up your clean bit, rinsed and toweled dry. Thread the end of the cheekpieces through the bit loops **(E)**. Bend the end of the leather and push through the first keeper below the hook **(F)**, followed by the second keeper, jumping over the hook **(G & H)**. Now, push the hook through the slit on the

7 (A–I)

CHAPTER 7 / *Tack Cleaning*

99

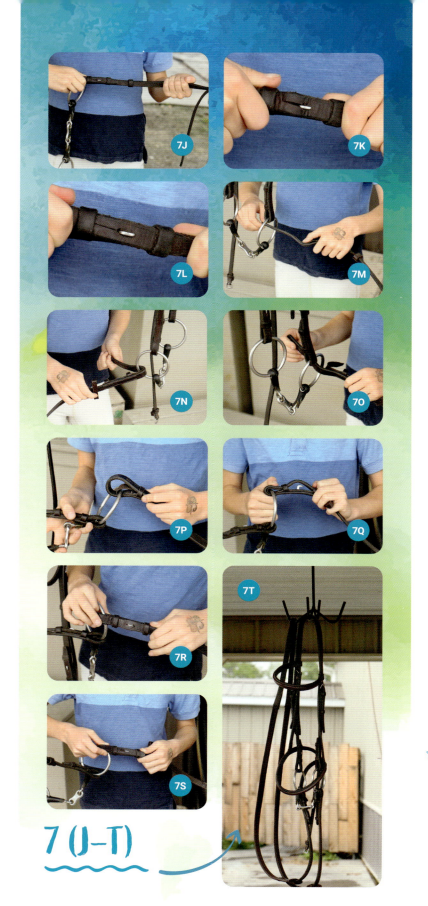

7 (J–T)

leather **(I)**. Then pull the folded end while firmly holding the cheekpiece **(J)**. You are looking for the hook to sit in the slightly wider end of the slit, so the slit closes and lies flat **(K & L)**. Repeat this on the other side, making sure the bit hangs with the curve facing up and back, then you connect the reins **(M)**. If your bridle has an extra piece of leather at the end of the reins, make sure it is lying with the main part of the rein **(N)**. If it is separated it will not lie flat inside the fold **(O)**. Make sure all keepers are correctly in place. Push the small piece through the keeper first, then the main piece over it **(P)**. Hop the hook to go through the second keeper **(Q)**. Push the hook through the slit **(R)** then pull to tighten like you did with the cheekpieces **(S)**. Repeat with the other side, then check that the bridle is correctly put back together before using **(T)**.

Storing Bridle

☆**8 A–H** If you have a period of time in the year when you are not riding, or if you have spare/old tack you want to keep, use Ko-Cho-Line® Leather Dressing to stop the leather from getting dried out or moldy **(A)**. This

THE KID'S GUIDE TO HORSEMANSHIP AND GROOMING / Cat Hill & Emma Ford

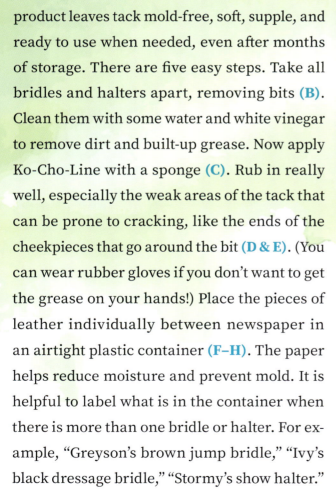

8 (A–H)

product leaves tack mold-free, soft, supple, and ready to use when needed, even after months of storage. There are five easy steps. Take all bridles and halters apart, removing bits **(B)**. Clean them with some water and white vinegar to remove dirt and built-up grease. Now apply Ko-Cho-Line with a sponge **(C)**. Rub in really well, especially the weak areas of the tack that can be prone to cracking, like the ends of the cheekpieces that go around the bit **(D & E)**. (You can wear rubber gloves if you don't want to get the grease on your hands!) Place the pieces of leather individually between newspaper in an airtight plastic container **(F–H)**. The paper helps reduce moisture and prevent mold. It is helpful to label what is in the container when there is more than one bridle or halter. For example, "Greyson's brown jump bridle," "Ivy's black dressage bridle," "Stormy's show halter."

CHAPTER 7 / Tack Cleaning

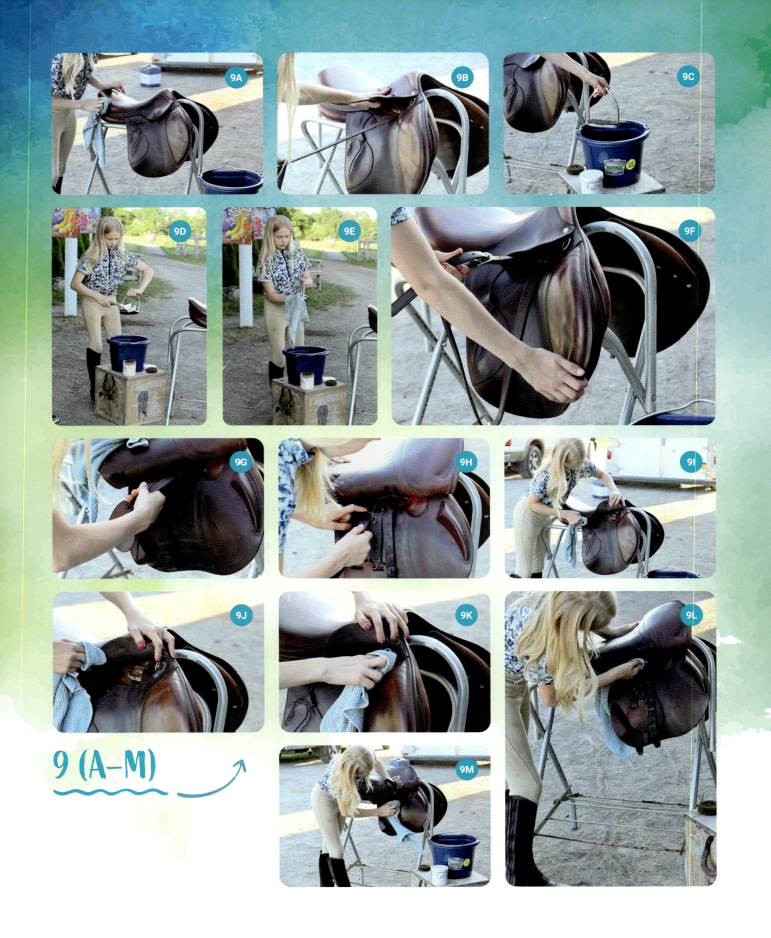

9 (A–M)

THE KID'S GUIDE TO HORSEMANSHIP AND GROOMING / Cat Hill & Emma Ford

102

PRO TIP
Brush It Clean

Use an old toothbrush to remove dirt within the folds of leather.

Saddle

Saddles are subjected to less sweat and dirt than bridles, which can make it tempting to overlook them when cleaning. But, just like your bridle, you need to make sure that you are caring for this important piece of equipment carefully.

Cleaning

☆**9 A–M** Wipe off any sweat and dirt with a damp towel every day **(A)**. Every seven or eight rides, do a good clean and condition. Pull off the stirrup leathers **(B)**. Wash the stirrup irons by placing them in some soapy water then scrubbing with a stiff bristled brush **(C & D)**. Wipe them dry with a towel **(E)**. Double-check the stitching by the buckle of the leathers **(F)**. Under the saddle flap, pull hard on the billets and check any stitching to make sure that the billets are still well attached **(G & H)**. When wiping away dirt and grease, get under every flap and around the dees **(I–M)** You may see black spots on the leather, and these are easily removed with your fingernail or a Scrub Daddy® sponge.

Conditioning and Storage

☆**10 A–J (next page)** As with the bridle, condition the saddle all over, starting with the seat and flaps **(A)**. Get underneath the flap that covers the stirrup bar **(B)**. Lift the flaps and get all the nooks and crannies **(C)**. Once you have everything conditioned and cleaned, thread the stirrup leather through the hole at the top of the stirrup **(D)**. Buckle the stirrup leather **(E)**. It is easier to put the stirrup back on most saddles if you push the loop over the stirrup bar, rather than trying to thread the leather up from the bottom **(F)**. Pull the bottom part of the leather until the buckle is at the top **(G & H)**.

CHAPTER 7 / *Tack Cleaning*

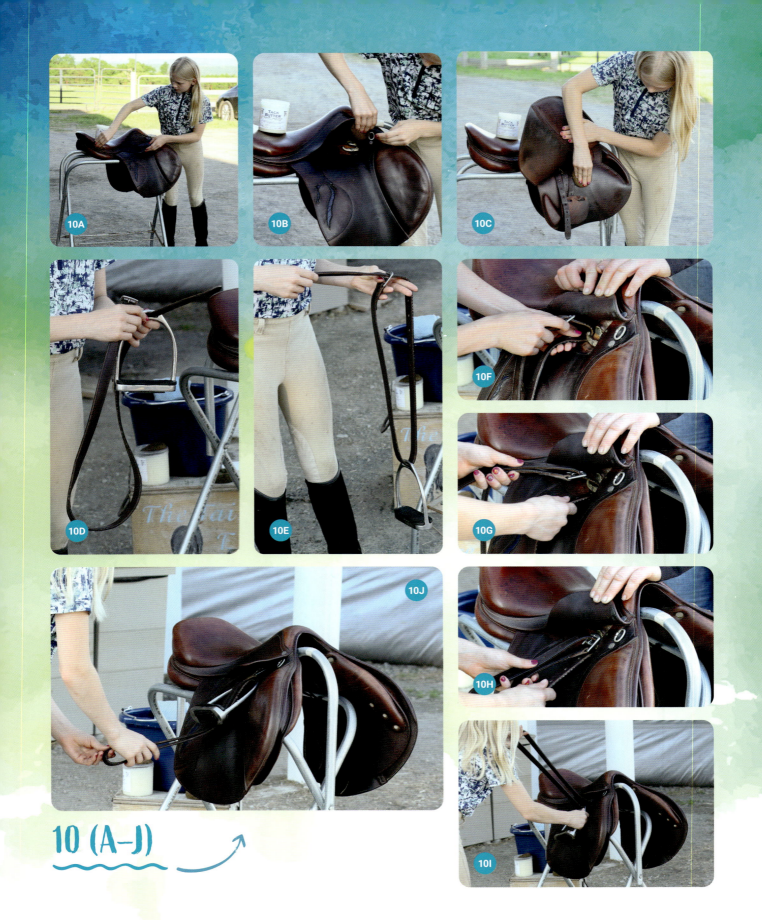

10 (A–J)

THE KID'S GUIDE TO HORSEMANSHIP AND GROOMING / Cat Hill & Emma Ford

Run the stirrup up the bottom leather **(I)**, and tuck the leather through the stirrup for storage **(J)**. For the panels of the saddle to remain in good shape, store the saddle on a solid saddle rack. The metal racks that have holes in them will—over time—misshape the saddle's panels, which leads to an ill-fitting saddle. If you have a metal rack, a simple fix is to buy a piece of 4-inch foam at the craft store, or a memory foam pillow, and set your saddle on top of it.

Girth

How you clean your girth depends on its material.

☆**11 A–D** *Fleece* girths should be brushed off after every ride with a stiff brush and allowed to air dry, preferably in the sun **(A)**. Depending how sweaty or wet the girth gets, it will need to be washed with a gentle detergent either by hand or in the washing machine. (Ask permission first!) All *leather* girths should be wiped clean and conditioned daily to prevent cracking. First, wipe any hair, dirt, and sweat off with a damp towel **(B)**. Then, use a conditioner on a clean sponge to keep the leather soft and prevent cracks **(C)**. Finally, check your stitching and elastic daily **(D)**. If your girth breaks, it is a very dangerous situation for all involved! *Neoprene* girths should be hosed off and allowed to dry slowly every day. Drying too fast causes early cracking of the material.

11 (A–D)

end of chapter 7

chapter eight

Travel Preparation:
Equipment and Trailer Loading

Travel Preparation: Equipment and Trailer Loading

One of the most fun and exciting things to do with your pony is take him on a trip. Going to a horse show, pony club rally, or clinic can be a great goal to work toward. It adds a whole new level of difficulty, though, because you need to be organized and prepared in order to have a great experience.

The best way to get yourself ready is to start by making lists! Lists help you organize all your needs. We have included a few list examples here, but they are no means all inclusive. You need to build your lists based on what you are doing and where you are going.

First, divide your list into sections. For example: *Pony Care, Tack, My Stuff.* Then, divide those into smaller lists. Under Pony Care, you might include: *1 bale of hay, 15 lbs. grain, 3 scoops electrolytes, water bucket.*

In this way, you end up with a full list of supplies that looks about like this:

PACKING LISTS
One-Day Show

☺Pony Care

- ✓ Water
- ✓ Water bucket
- ✓ 1 bale hay
- ✓ Hay net
- ✓ Emergency medical kit
- ✓ Extra lead rope
- ✓ Extra halter
- ✓ Wash/rinse bucket

☺Tack

- ✓ Saddle
- ✓ Bridle
- ✓ Saddle pad
- ✓ Girth

☺Event Supplies

- ✓ Pinny holder
- ✓ Safety pins
- ✓ Medical armband

☺Paperwork

- ✓ Coggins
- ✓ Vaccination history
- ✓ Stall card

☺Trailer Setup

- ✓ Saddle rack
- ✓ Hooks
- ✓ Double end snaps
- ✓ Laundry bag
- ✓ Extra twine

☺My Stuff

- ✓ Helmet
- ✓ Show clothes (pants, jacket, shirt, gloves)
- ✓ Extra coverups
- ✓ Boots
- ✓ Water
- ✓ Snacks

CHAPTER 8 / Travel Preparation: Equipment and Trailer Loading

PACKING LISTS
Overnight Trip

☺ Pony Care

- ✓ Water
- ✓ Two water buckets
- ✓ Two bales hay
- ✓ Hay net
- ✓ 5 pounds grain
- ✓ Grain bucket
- ✓ Blanket
- ✓ Cooler
- ✓ Leg wraps
- ✓ Emergency medical kit
- ✓ Extra lead rope
- ✓ Extra halter

☺ Tack

- ✓ Saddle
- ✓ Bridle
- ✓ Saddle pad
- ✓ Girth

☺ Event Supplies

- ✓ Pinny holder
- ✓ Safety pins
- ✓ Medical armband

☺ Paperwork

- ✓ Coggins
- ✓ Vaccination history
- ✓ Stall card

☺ Barn Setup

- ✓ 4 bags bedding
- ✓ Stall guard
- ✓ Saddle rack
- ✓ Hooks
- ✓ Double end snaps
- ✓ Laundry bag
- ✓ Extra twine

☺ My Stuff

- ✓ Helmet
- ✓ Casual clothes
- ✓ Pajamas
- ✓ Show clothes (pants, jacket, shirt, gloves)
- ✓ Extra coverups
- ✓ Boots
- ✓ Water
- ✓ Snacks

THE KID'S GUIDE TO HORSEMANSHIP AND GROOMING / Cat Hill & Emma Ford

Packing

Once you have your lists made, go around your barn and make sure everything is clean before you pack it! Then take everything out and organize it into piles by the groups your list created.

☆ **1 A–G** When packing, think about what you will need when you get to the competition. It may help you to write all this down **(A)**! Most phones also have a great list function. We use the Google Keep App that allows you to check off a list as you go **(B)**. First, you want to see to your pony's comfort. Do you have hay and water ready and accessible? We recommend carrying 10 gallons of water for a day show just in case you can't get water or the water on site isn't suitable for drinking. Do you have a small bucket you can lift to your pony to offer water? If you are staying on site, you will also need big buckets and a grain tub or bucket. You will need your grooming kit to brush your pony. And your tack. When you are competing with different tack throughout the competition, check your show schedule and see which classes or division you do first, second, and so on. After that you need the supplies for pony aftercare. As you go through your list, carefully lay everything out near your trunk **(C)**. Once you have your schedule written down, work backward to pack, so the stuff you need last goes in the trunk first **(D)**. Large items that don't fit in the trunk can be set right next to it **(E)**. Once you have all the supplies out, pack your horse trailer backward. The stuff you need last goes in first, and the last things to be loaded are what you need immediately upon arrival. This way, once you are all done, you have your stuff right at hand when you get there and avoid

1 (A–B)

CHAPTER 8 / Travel Preparation: Equipment and Trailer Loading

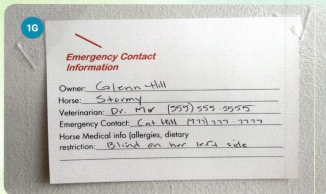

1 (C–G)

the dreaded "digging through the trailer"! **(F)**. Make sure you have an emergency card with your pony's information clearly posted in the horse trailer or on a stall. This card should have the pony's name, and pertinent medical information, an emergency contact (ideally a trainer, barn owner, or other horse-knowledgeable person), your veterinarian, and your contact information. This is the best way for your pony to stay safe while on the road **(G)**!

"Just in Case"

Pack for the "just in case." Lugging around a bunch of stuff you never need is always better than needing emergency supplies and not having them. You should always have a spare halter and lead rope.

☆ **2 A–E** Bring a horse medical kit containing: leg bandages, Vetrap, gauze, Elastikon bandage tape, antibiotic ointment, betadine, and alcohol **(A & B)**. Your human medical kit should include: band-aids, Benadryl, ice packs, antibiotic ointment, alcohol wipes, gauze, and an ace bandage **(C & D)**. Have an emergency kit with duct tape, string or twine, a hammer, a wrench, bungee cords, and WD-40. And every horse trailer should always have a trailer jack, wheel chocks **(E)**, a tire iron that fits the

THE KID'S GUIDE TO HORSEMANSHIP AND GROOMING / *Cat Hill & Emma Ford* trailer lug-nuts, and a fire extinguisher. Once you've packed your trailer and made sure you have all your emergency supplies, move on to your pony.

Pony Leg Protection While Traveling

When traveling away from home, keeping your horse or pony safe on the trailer, no matter how long or short the trip, is most important. There are many options available to help you and your pony have a safe trip, as well as how to correctly load and unload your pony.

When it comes to protective clothing for your pony, you have a few choices, from no protection at all to full head-to-tail gear. It does help if you can ask someone who has shipped your horse previously what travel equipment was used. However, when this is not an option, put on the travelwear you intend to use (for example, shipping boots), and let your horse move around his stall with it on before you attempt to load him on the trailer.

Option 1: No Additional Protection

☆**3 (next page)** If your pony has no shoes and is known to travel well, no protection is perfectly fine. Stormy wears front shoes only, and she is an experienced traveler. No additional protection is the right choice for her.

2 (A–E)

CHAPTER 8 / Travel Preparation: Equipment and Trailer Loading

113

Option 2: Bell Boots Only

If your pony wears shoes, it might be a good idea to put on bell boots to prevent him from stepping on himself and cutting his coronary band. On extremely hot days, less protection can be better for the horse. This option gives you the basic protection while keeping him cool.

☆**4** You can do just the front feet or all four. Arther wears four shoes but is a fairly quiet shipper, so bell boots are the right choice for him on a hot day (see p. 66 for instructions on how to put them on).

Option 3: Shipping Boots

These come in various materials, colors, and shapes. Ideally, use boots that go above the knees and hocks. The material should be sturdy enough so it does not slide down your pony's legs, which can frighten him, causing him to kick or slip in the trailer.

Front Boots

☆**5 A–H** To put *front* shipping boots on, stand facing the leg at the shoulder **(A)**. Run your hand down your pony's leg to let him know you will be working in that area. Holding the boot in the middle, open up the boot and place

THE KID'S GUIDE TO HORSEMANSHIP AND GROOMING / Cat Hill & Emma Ford

it around the leg at about knee height with the straps on the inside **(B)**. You always want to start a bit higher so you can smooth the hair in the correct direction as you put the boot in place. Slide the boot down the leg until it is barely touching the floor **(C)**. If there are three straps, take the middle strap, and pull across the front then around the side toward the tail **(D)**. It should be snug. Repeat this step with the remaining straps—first the lower straps, then the top ones **(E–H)**.

Hind Boots

☆**6 A–J (next page)** When doing the *hind* boots always let your pony know you are going to be working on that leg **(A)**. Starting at the rump, run your hand down his leg. As with the front boots, slide the boot into position **(B & C)**.

CHAPTER 8 / *Travel Preparation: Equipment and Trailer Loading*

6 (A–J)

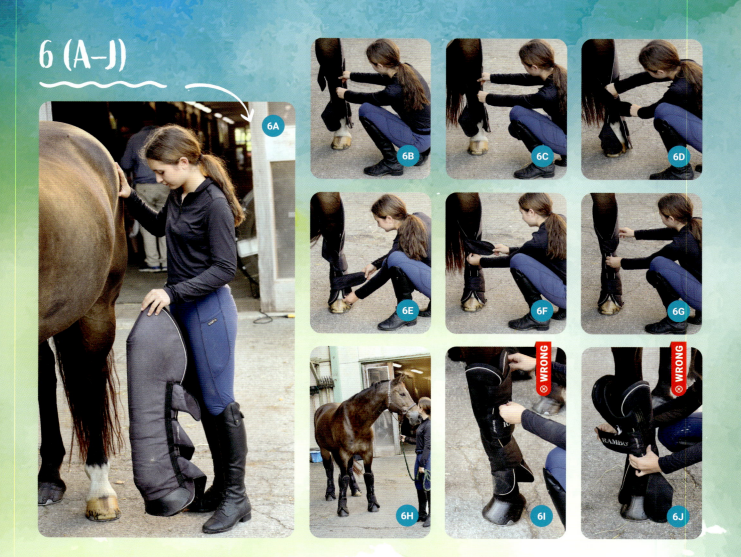

Do the middle strap first, followed by the lower strap, then the top strap **(D–H)**. Arther wears four shoes, and is a fairly quiet shipper, but on a cool day shipping boots are the right choice for him. Common mistakes with shipping boots include when the Velcro is done up on the outside, rather than pulling straps across the front **(I)** and when the straps are pulled to inside rather than across the front to the outside **(J)**.

THE KID'S GUIDE TO HORSEMANSHIP AND GROOMING / Cat Hill & Emma Ford

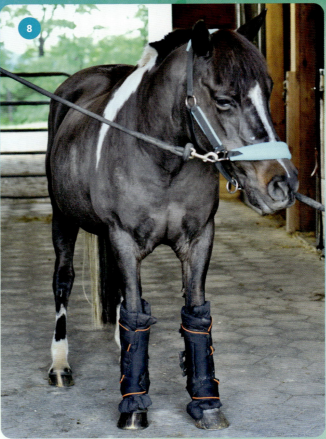

Option 4: Shipping Bandages

Some horses do better with bandages for trailering. It is very important that the wraps are applied correctly. When put on too loose or too tight, you can damage your horse's legs so, if needed, an adult with experienced wrapping skills should apply the wraps for you. It takes hundreds of practice rounds to get good enough at wrapping legs to leave the wraps on for trailering.

☆7 Greyson shows a normal standing wrap with a bell boot for protection on the right front leg, and a shipping bandage wrap on the left front leg.

Option 5: All-in-One Wraps

These wraps have been on the market for a few years now, and there are various kinds with different therapeutic properties to them, like improved circulation, without a huge amount of additional heat.

☆8 We like the Horseware® Rambo® Ionic wraps that are shown here. Stormy, after working hard at a show, likes to have Ionic wraps for the ride home to help her tired legs feel better. Now that you have the legs protected, what else needs protection when shipping your pony?

CHAPTER 8 / Travel Preparation: Equipment and Trailer Loading

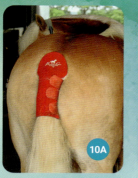

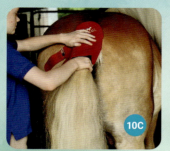

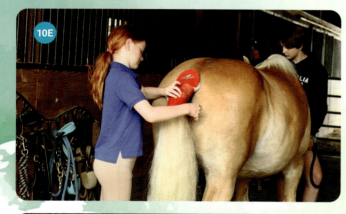
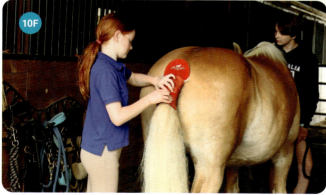

10 (A–F)

Heads and Tails

Head Protection

☆**9** A head bumper is a "cap" that fits over the horse's ears and is secured by the halter to protect his poll should he hit his head while loading or traveling. It is normally made from a very thick felt material covered in leather.

Tail Protection

When your horse rubs his tail while shipping, or if you have a pulled or braided tail to protect, you might want to apply a velcro tail wrap.

☆**10 A–F** Velcro wraps as modeled by Milka are fairly easy to apply **(A)**. They come in various lengths. First, gather up all the hair at the top of the tail **(B)**. Milka has a lot of tail! Place the

THE KID'S GUIDE TO HORSEMANSHIP AND GROOMING / Cat Hill & Emma Ford

wrap at the top of the dock **(C)**. The top strap should be pulled underneath in a clockwise direction as close to the top of the tail as possible **(D)**. Repeat with the remaining straps, making sure you capture all the tail hairs within the wrap as you go **(E & F)**.

Blanket or Cooler

The final decision you need to make for trailering is the type of blanket or cooler you may want to use. This depends on the weather. Throughout most of the summer months your pony will be most comfortable without any covering. However, in the colder months, you will need to decide how to keep him warm.

☆**11** When your horse is still a bit wet at the time you want to load, you need to layer so he can dry off and not have a damp blanket next to his skin. This process is known as *wicking*. Using an Irish knit as a bottom layer with a fleece or wool cooler on top is ideal for this purpose.

☆**12 A & B** You must make sure that any blankets you use have correct front closures and a correctly fitted belly surcingle **(A & B)**. You do not want the blanket twisting around your horse's belly and causing panic.

☆**13** Greyson is ready to load with his head bumper, net cooler, ionic boots, and bell boots for protection.

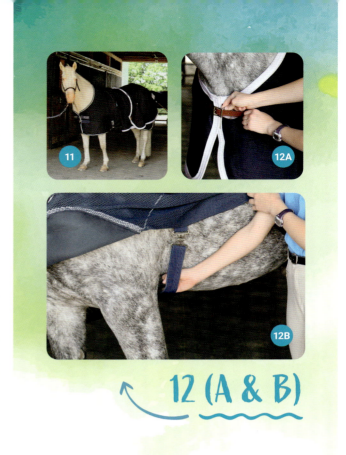

12 (A & B)

CHAPTER 8 / *Travel Preparation: Equipment and Trailer Loading*

14 (A–F)

Preparing to Load

Loading your pony onto a trailer must not be rushed! Always have an adult helper with you. If you have never trailered your pony or it's been a long time since he has been loaded, it is always a good idea to have a practice run earlier in the week, if time permits, before trying to go somewhere. Leave yourself longer than you think you will need to load your pony. A nervous horse senses when you are rushing and often gets scared. Before you start loading you will need to ask an adult to check the following:

☆ **14 A–F** The trailer must be correctly attached to the ball on the towing vehicle, the safety chains in place **(A)**, the electric and brake systems properly connected and working **(B)**, and windows of the trailer opened for ventilation **(C)**. The tires should have enough pressure **(D)**. The adult should double-check that

THE KID'S GUIDE TO HORSEMANSHIP AND GROOMING / Cat Hill & Emma Ford

15 (A–E)

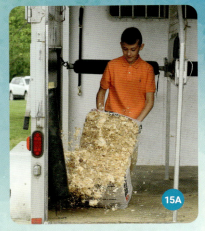
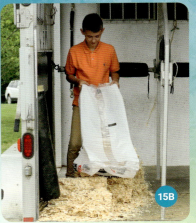

a jack, wheel chocks, lug wrench, and small fire extinguisher are easily accessible in the trailer or towing vehicle **(E & F)**.

Setting up the Trailer

Trailer floors can rot if they get too wet, so it's important to clean and empty a trailer between uses.

☆**15 A–G** When it's time to go, bed the trailer with plenty of shavings or the bedding you use in your pony's stall **(A–C)**. Hang a hay net up high enough so your pony can't get his feet stuck in it **(D)**. It's always a good idea to tie the hay net to a piece of string rather than directly to the

CHAPTER 8 / *Travel Preparation: Equipment and Trailer Loading*

trailer in case it does need to break away easily **(E)**. You should always carry clean drinking water, even on a short trailer ride, because should there be a delay on the way, you need to be able to give your pony a drink. Fill the jug from your horse's normal drinking water source **(F)**. Have an adult help carry it to the trailer, and secure it where it can't tip over **(G)**. Have a small bucket for offering water to your horse in the trailer, too.

Before loading, open up a front side door so you can get out easily. Ensure the breast bar is securely fastened. If there is a ramp, it must be fully down and touching the ground evenly. The butt bar should be down and not swinging. You are now ready to get your pony! Ask your parent or helper to stand close to the ramp on the driver's side, if shipping one horse, and explain that you need him or her to put up the butt bar once your pony is on completely.

Loading

☆**16 A–H** Ask your pony to walk next you. You can see here that Stormy is walking beside Glenn, not dragging behind as they approach **(A)**. Make sure you are walking to the middle of the trailer stall and *not* to the middle partition. This means you should be slightly left of center on the driver's side **(B)**. Stay by your pony's head and walk with him straight up to the chest bar; duck and go under the bar as he puts his head over it **(C)**. Ask your helper to put the butt bar up **(D)**.

THE KID'S GUIDE TO HORSEMANSHIP AND GROOMING / Cat Hill & Emma Ford

122

16 (A–H)

Stand by your pony's head as the butt bar is closed **(E)**. Only after this is done do you connect the trailer tie to his halter **(F)** and unclip the lead rope **(G)**. Tying your pony up before the butt bar is secure can lead to a very bad situation should he decide to exit the trailer backward in a panic. Once Stormy is tied up, Glenn hops out the side door and helps to put the ramp up. Double-check that windows are open for ventilation and all side and top doors are securely locked into position **(H)**. Safe travels!

CHAPTER 8 / Travel Preparation: Equipment and Trailer Loading

123

chapter nine

Care at a Show or Clinic

9

Care at a Show or Clinic

You have arrived!

Once you reach your destination, first check on your horse, and on warm days, especially, latch the side door back open to allow for more airflow. Organize your tack, grooming equipment and personal riding clothes before unloading your horse.

Unloading

☆**1 A–L** Attach the lead rope and untie your pony **(A)**. Ask your helper to slowly lower the ramp, then step to the driver's side and lower the butt bar **(B & C)**. Gently ask your pony to walk slowly backward as you duck under the chest bar **(D)**. Keep him straight until you are completely off the ramp **(E & F)**.

Using a quick release knot tied to string (see p. 17 for instructions), you can now tie him to the side of the trailer. Do not tie too short or too long **(G & H)**. Think about tying a little more than an arm's length from the trailer **(I)**. Tie short enough so he can move his head to look around and eat

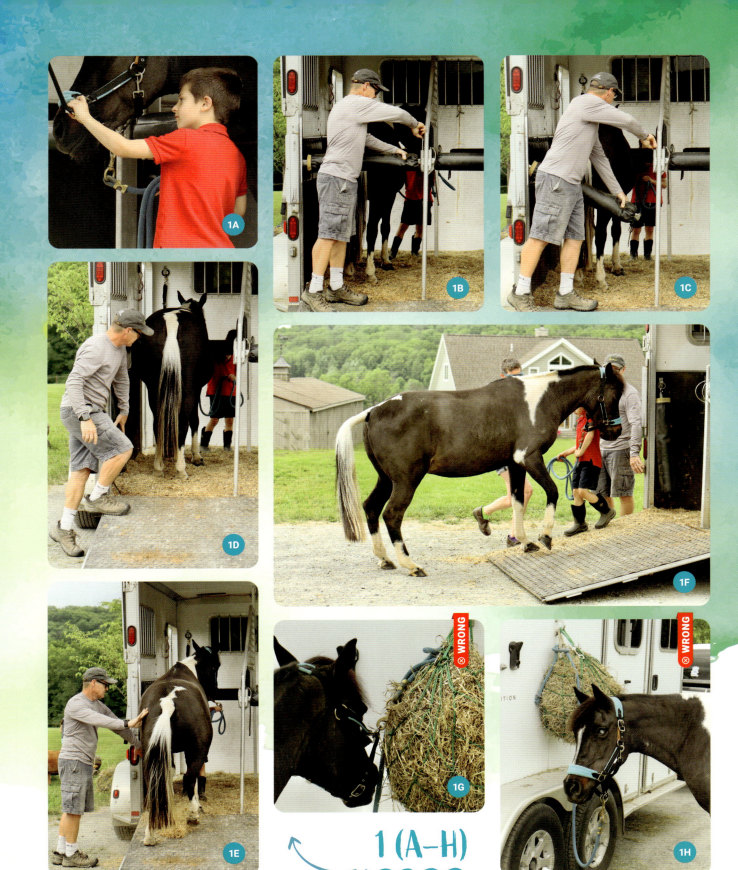

1 (A–H)

CHAPTER 9 / Care at a Show or Clinic

127

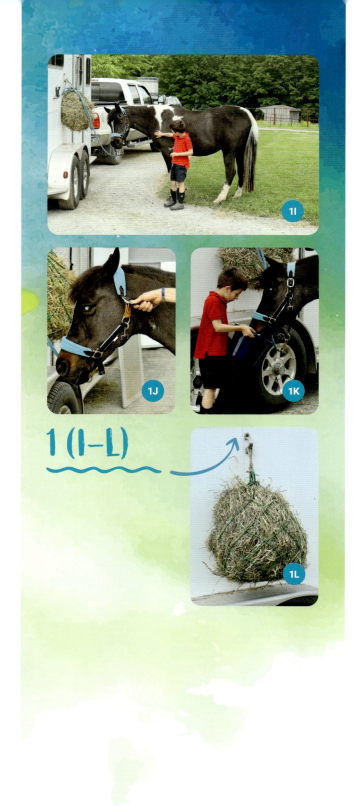

1 (I–L)

hay comfortably, but not too long he could get his leg over the lead rope and panic if he steps back. Using a halter with its own breakaway method is a good idea. Stormy's halter has a piece of leather attached to the middle ring and buckle that will break if she panics **(J)**. Tie a hay net up within reach, then offer him some water **(K)**. Remember to keep all buckets, equipment, and hay nets safely out of the way of his feet **(L)**. Never leave your pony alone at the trailer; an adult should always be present. If you decide to put him back on the trailer in between rides, always put up the back ramp. Ponies can do the craziest things and backing out under the butt bar has happened! When you arrive at your destination, whether it is a show, lesson or Pony Club rally, it is important to take care of your horse first. It is very easy to get sidetracked by your friends and the other entertainment going on; however, *your horse should always come first*. We are going to talk about how to make your horse comfortable and run your day efficiently so you can get the most out of it. You need to set up your equipment so everything is in easy reach but safe from any hooves! This is where the good packing skills you learned in chapter 8 (p. 108) come in handy.

Setting Up Equipment

☆ **2 A–E** Provided the weather is good, having a collapsible saddle rack to keep your saddle, saddle pads, girths, and half pads outside but

off the ground is a convenient solution **(A)**. If your tack room door does not have hooks to hang your bridle, lay it over the top of your saddle **(B)**. Bring your tack trunk outside, then set up some water buckets **(C)**. Keep one just for drinking water and have at least two available for cooling down when necessary. If you have specific ride times, make sure you give yourself plenty of time to tack up. Your horse will need to be groomed, his feet picked and oiled, and mane and tail brushed out. Put the saddle and boots on your pony before you get yourself ready. Remove the hay net before you get dressed so your pony can empty his mouth. Once you are fully dressed, you can put on the bridle. Remember to hang the halter up after you take it off. Do not leave it just dangling to the ground **(D & E)**.

Cooling Out

☆ **3 A–C (next page)** Once you've finished riding, cool out your horse properly—you can see Ivy still has flared nostrils and her veins are standing out **(A)**. Ivy needs

CHAPTER 9 / *Care at a Show or Clinic*

3 (A–C)

to do more walking before returning to the trailer and getting washed down. When your pony feels cool to the touch and his breathing is normal, remove all tack, offer him a drink, then have a friend hold him away from the trailer so you can bucket wash him (see p. 72 on how to bucket rinse). Scrape and towel him off well; then, if possible, take him where he can eat some grass and dry in the sun. When it's very hot, try to find a shady area with a breeze **(B)**. Once he's dry, offer him another drink, re-tie him to the trailer, give him a hay net, and if you are done for the day, start to put away your equipment. Dunk your bit in a bucket of water so that the slobber doesn't dry hard onto the metal **(C)**. Before loading back onto the trailer, give your pony a curry and brush down, checking for any cuts or abrasions. Put on any travel equipment. Offer water one last time before loading.

Things to Remember at One-Day Shows and Clinics

☺ *Do pay attention to weather and make sure you and your pony have the correct clothes for the conditions.*

☺ *Do park in the shade if you can and find a breeze on very hot days.*

☺ *Do tie up your pony to the trailer with a quick-release knot.*

☺ *Do offer him water on a regular basis.*

☺ *Do thank the volunteers, instructors, and office people before leaving.*

☺ *Do make sure your pony is completely cooled down before reloading for home.*

☺ *Do NOT leave your pony alone tied up at the trailer.*

☺ *Do NOT tie the lead rope straight to metal; use string at the end of the rope to ensure it will break should the horse panic and pull back.*

☺ *Do NOT put your pony on the trailer to stand for a long time without adequate ventilation, hay, and water.*

Stabling Overnight

The likelihood is that your pony is used to a lot of paddock time at home. When stabling overnight somewhere, you need to make sure the stall is comfortable for your pony, as well as making a well-thought-out plan so you have plenty of time to hand-graze your pony during the day.

When you first get to the destination and find your stall, make a decision on how to set it up. In tent stabling, it is best to hang your water buckets then let your pony graze down the stall. If you put the bedding down first, he will only dig it up to find the grass!

When stabled in a permanent barn, put down bedding and hang water buckets before putting him in the stall.

To bed down the stall, when using shavings, you will need about four bags of shavings.

☆ **4 A–I** Using scissors to cut halfway down the bag is easiest **(A & B)**. Holding the top of the bag, use your knee to push the shavings bag in half **(C)**. Then you can lift the bag from the top and the shavings should release themselves pretty easily **(D & E)**. Next, take a pitchfork and break up the shavings,

4 (A–I)

shaking or throwing clumps into the air to separate them **(E–G)**. Once you have shaken out the clumps, smooth out the bed to lie flat **(H)**, and sweep back the front of the stall to look neat and tidy **(I)**.

☆ **5** Water buckets can be hung from a piece of bailing twine or from an over-the-wall bucket hook. When hanging a hay net, always tie to a piece of string and high enough so your pony can't catch a pawing hoof in it.

☆ **6 A & B** Remember, there are probably a lot of people needing to do the same things as you, so try to work efficiently and quickly to offload

THE KID'S GUIDE TO HORSEMANSHIP AND GROOMING / Cat Hill & Emma Ford

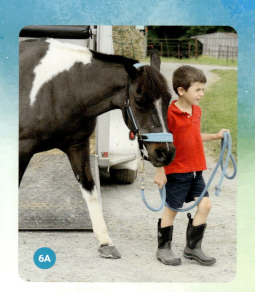

your pony and equipment. There will be plenty of time to catch up with friends later!

Setting Up Equipment for Overnight

☆ **7 A–E (next page)** Once your pony has had a walk and there is plenty of hay and water in his stall, you can now set up your area, hanging your tack and tidying your space **(A)**. Hang a clean towel over the stall and then place a bridle hook on top **(B & C)**. Use the hook for your bridle, breastplate (optional), long girth, halter, and lead rope **(D)**. Your halter should be hung from both side rings, with the noseband closer to the top. Your lead rope should be rolled and placed on top of your halter. (To correctly roll your lead rope, see page 27.) Blankets should be folded neatly on a piece of string or chain stall guard attached to the front of the stall door. Try to minimize your equipment to one or two trunks that can be stacked neatly in front of your stall **(E)**.

CHAPTER 9 / *Care at a Show or Clinic*

133

7 (A–E)

THINGS TO REMEMBER
When Overnighting

- Do hang buckets and feeders with string for easy breakaway.

- Do hang hay nets high enough off the floor to stay clear of rolling or pawing feet.

- Do walk your horse as soon as the trailer has been parked.

- Do take note of how much he is drinking. Write it down if necessary.

- Do keep things tidy in the aisle. Remember, other people and horses need to pass.

- Do keep trunk latches shut correctly when not in use to prevent horses catching and injuring their legs on them.

- Do take your pony on regular walks and hand-grazing outings.

- Do place an information card on the stall in case of an emergency.

- ALWAYS double latch the door at night. Ponies can be great escape artists when they choose to be.

- Do NOT leave your pony unattended with the door open.

- Do NOT put your pony away if he is not fully cooled out.

- Do NOT leave your halter dangling from the wall or stall front where it might become a hazard to other horses.

- Do NOT feed grain meals too close to your riding time. Give him at least one to two hours to digest his grain.

CHAPTER 9 / Care at a Show or Clinic

135

PRO TIP
Keeping Your Horse Comfortable at a Show

Going to any show—whether for a day or overnight—can be very stressful for your horse. Listen to what he is trying to tell you by carefully watching his behavior. This attention is essential to good care.

One of the biggest dangers for the traveling horse is insufficient water intake. Soaking the hay, wetting grain, and hand-grazing are three ways to help increase water intake.

When the days are super-hot or your pony is a bit older, the use of Flair™ Equine Nasal Strips can be useful to help him cool down. A Flair Strip is like a band-aid with a stiff piece of

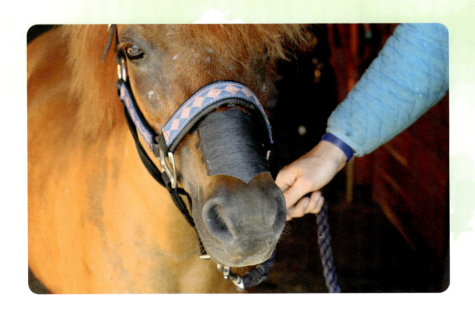

plastic in it. When applied correctly, it opens up the nasal passage of the horse so he can take in more oxygen. This one item alone can help your partner recover from a big exertion faster, which means a less stressful time for you and your pony. Posy has allergies, and often struggles to catch her breath when working hard. Flair Strips help her continue to be active and useful as she ages. We use them whenever she's going out for longer or faster speed rides.

Remember, hand-grazing is a great way to keep your pony happy when in a new place. As long as you have space between you, it's also a good chance to socialize with friends while being nice to your horse!

chapter ten

Pony Glow Up

Pony Glow Up

*Taking your horse on an outing
means spending a little extra time getting him
as beautifully turned out as you can.
In this chapter, we will teach you how to give him
that extra special touch to make him sparkle.
Whether you are taking your horse
to a lesson, clinic, or horse show,
you want to start with an extra tidy up.*

A day or two before the special event, groom as you would every day and take stock of where your horse needs some extra attention. Is his face a little furry? How clean is he? How is his mane and tail looking?

Clipping

When his face is a little fuzzy, you can clip the long "goat hairs" and trim the bridle path.

☆ **1 A–F** Any time you're using clippers, first show them to your horse while they are turned off so you don't startle him **(A)**. Then, still holding them ahead of the horse and a bit to the

1 (A–F)

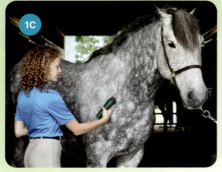

side (remember the blind spot right in front of his nose!), go ahead and turn them on **(B)**. Check your horse's reaction. When he is calm, you can proceed, but if he seems nervous or upset, it's best to get a helper. Hold the running clippers in your hand and touch only your hand to his shoulder. Softly move the hand with the clippers back and forth a few inches low on the neck so he feels the vibration. Take a look at Greyson in these pictures: In the first he is a little unsure—his head is up, his ears are half back, and his eye is tight **(C)**. In the next, after just staying still and quiet for a few seconds, he is relaxed and has a cheerful expression, with his neck lowered, eyes bright and soft, and ears forward **(D)**. Once he is calm and happy, move to the face. Turn the clippers so the bottom of the blade faces you, and starting at the front of the horse's jowl, use the clippers in a stroking motion to brush down the hair **(E)**. Turn the clippers so the bottom of the blade faces the horse, and run the clippers along the bottom of the head toward his lips **(F)**. Repeat on the other side, then take a step away and check your work.

CHAPTER 10 / Pony Glow Up

141

Mane

Next, you can trim the bridle path, which is the area of the mane right behind the poll where the bridle sits. Your bridle path should only be two or three fingers wide, just wide enough for the bridle and halter to sit cleanly. Follow the previous steps ☆1 **A–F** to check that your horse is happy and comfortable with the clippers.

☆**2 A–D** Now, slide the halter back to hold the mane away from the hairs you want to cut **(A)**. Then place the clippers so the blade is flat on the horse's crest, and the points face the horse's withers **(B)**. Slide the clippers back until they just barely reach the long hairs held back by the halter **(C)**. Check your work and clean up if necessary **(D)**.

Banging the Tail

Working on the other end, it is time to clean up the tips of his tail. A nice, clean line makes him look freshly tidied up. First, comb the tail as shown on page 41.

☆**3 A–G** Once it's tangle-free, stand to the side of the horse's hindquarters and carefully smooth the hair from the dock down **(A)**. Gather the hair in one hand **(B)** and, trying not to lose any hairs, run your hand down to an inch or two from the very bottom of the tail **(C)**. Grasping the hair tightly **(D)**, cut a clean line

2 (A–D)

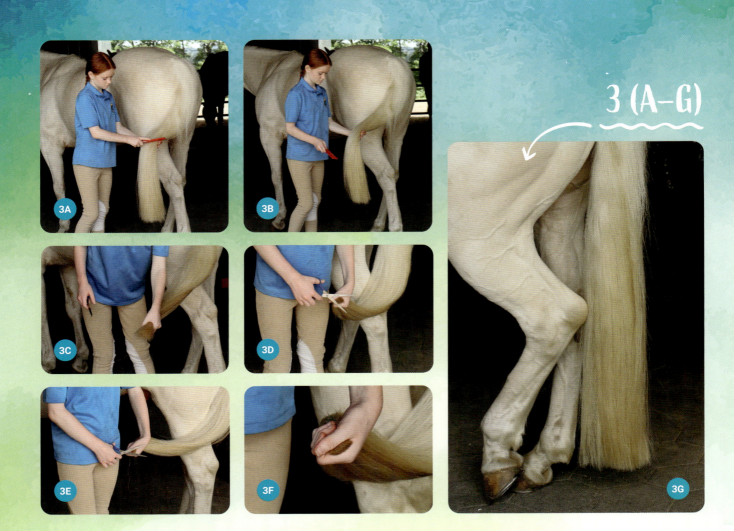

with scissors across the bottom **(E)**. You will need to comb out the tail a couple more times and check for missed hairs that may need trimming to complete a tidy look **(F & G)**.

Cleaning Manure Spots

Ideally, you get to give your horse a bath the day before or the morning before you leave (see p. 74). But what happens when, on the day of your special event, you show up to find your horse has rolled in a pile of manure? With no time to bathe, what do you do?

Don't panic, you can take care of this. The easiest is to have a bottle of dry shampoo on hand. If you don't have any, you can mix a couple of drops of purple shampoo into some alcohol to make a decent alternative.

☆ **4 A–C (next page)** Spray the manure spot with your cleaning mixture until it is soaked **(A)** and rub it really hard with a towel **(B)**. Check to see if the spot is clean **(C)**. When good, use the towel to smooth the hair flat; otherwise, repeat the scrubbing steps.

CHAPTER 10 / Pony Glow Up

143

4 (A–C)

Finishing Touches

Hoof Oil

Once your pony is groomed up, apply hoof oil to the outside of the hoof (see p. 43).

Tame That Mane

☆ **5 A & B** When his mane is a little wild, put a small amount of mousse or gel on your hands, rub it into his mane, and comb it down flat **(A)**. Take a slightly damp towel and drape it over his neck **(B)**. Straighten the towel out and let it sit for 10 to 15 minutes to help train the mane flat.

Shine His Coat

Putting a little oil on his coat will bring out the shine and show off his muscles and condition. We use Shapley's™ Light Oil No. 1. Do not use a detangler because it can make his coat slippery and cause your saddle to slip when you ride!

☆ **6 A–D** Use a fleece mitt, and spray the oil on the mitt, not his hair **(A)**. Starting at his neck, rub the oil onto his coat **(B)**. Finish it by smoothing his hair down with the mitt **(C)**. Use a towel with a little oil on it to wipe his nose and eyes and make the skin soft and shiny **(D)**.

THE KID'S GUIDE TO HORSEMANSHIP AND GROOMING / Cat Hill & Emma Ford

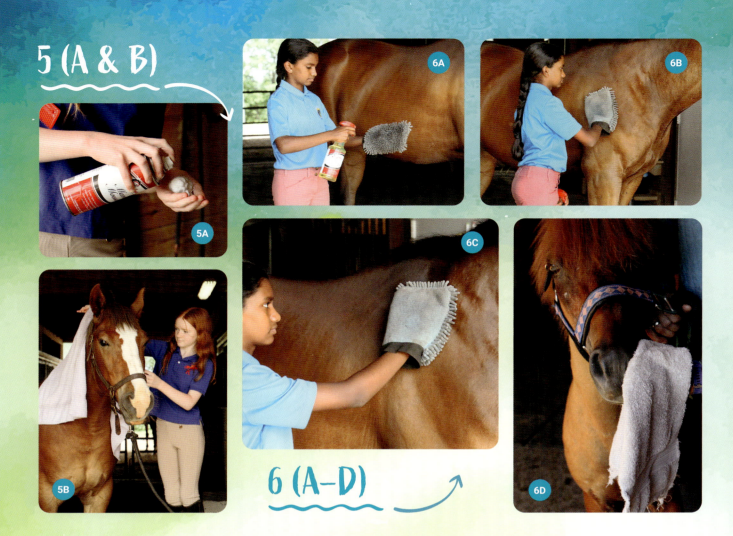

Dazzling Tail

To put a final extra polish on your horse, you can use a shine-enhancing spray on his tail.

☆ **7 A–C (next page)** First, standing to the side of the hip, lift his tail and fan it out **(A)**. Sweeping the can back and forth, then up and down, spray his tail **(B)**. Finish by carefully combing the tail from bottom to top **(C)**.

Quarter Marks

For a fun, fancy finish on the day of the event, you can learn how to do quarter marks.

Preparing for the Pattern

☆ **8 A–C (page 147)** You will need a short-bristle, medium-stiff brush, some fly spray or witch hazel in a spray bottle, and a stencil (optional)

CHAPTER 10 / *Pony Glow Up*

7 (A–C)

(A). When you are doing free-hand quarter marks, start by spraying the horse's hindquarters with the witch hazel until the entire area is damp (B). Smooth all the hair in the same direction with your brush (C).

Brushing the Pattern

☆ **9 A–K** Now, start the pattern. Hold the brush steady and put the front of the brush (by your fingertips) down on the hair **(A)**. You want the brush to travel on an angle from the top of his croup toward his hock, making a nice straight line **(B)**. Lift your brush and reposition it so it faces the other way, with the brush farther back on his croup and the bottom facing his stifle **(C)**. Drag the brush in a straight line toward his stifle **(D)** until it crosses the line you already made **(E)**. Lift your brush and put it parallel to the ground at the bottom of the "V" you just made **(F)**. Drag the brush on a straight line back toward his tail to square off the point of the "V" **(G)**. Turn your brush again and smooth all the hair from the "V" down so it's going the same direction again **(H)**. Being careful not to touch any of the area you have already done, reach up and put the brush on his spine right in front of his croup **(I)** and drag it along his spine until you reach his tail **(J)**. This completes one part of your quarter marks **(K)**.

THE KID'S GUIDE TO HORSEMANSHIP AND GROOMING / Cat Hill & Emma Ford

8 (A–C)

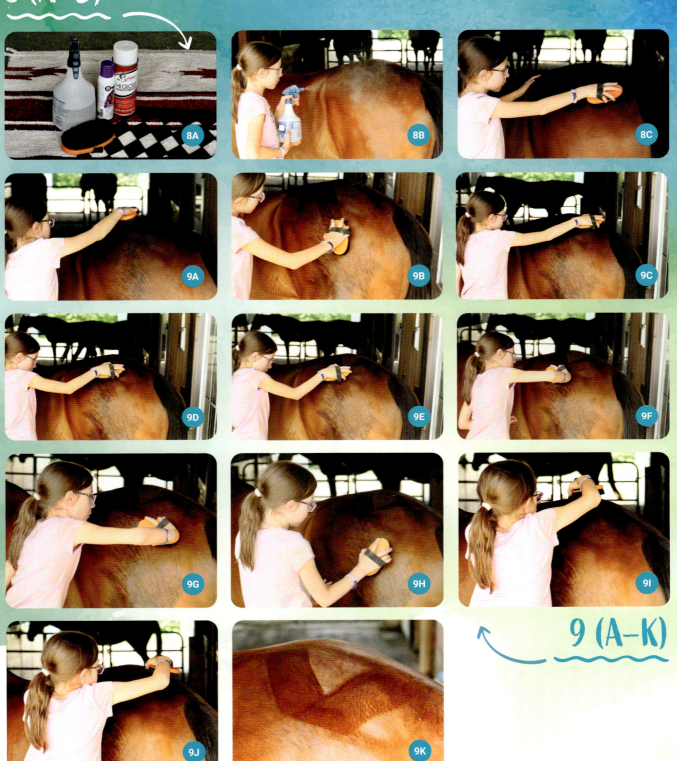

9 (A–K)

CHAPTER 10 / Pony Glow Up

147

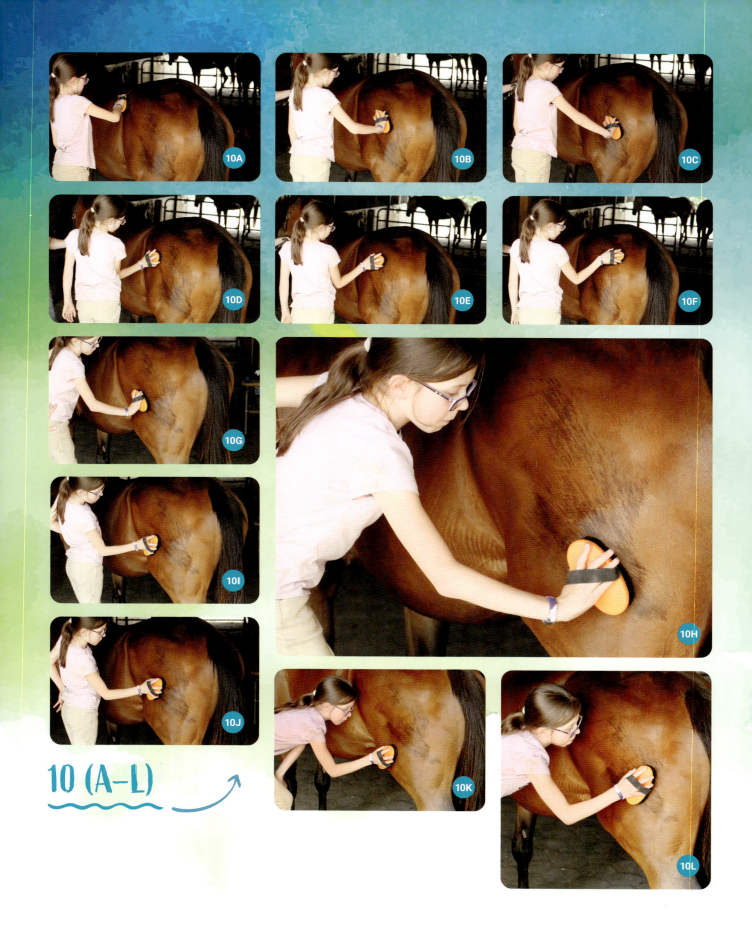

10 (A–L)

THE KID'S GUIDE TO HORSEMANSHIP AND GROOMING / Cat Hill & Emma Ford

148

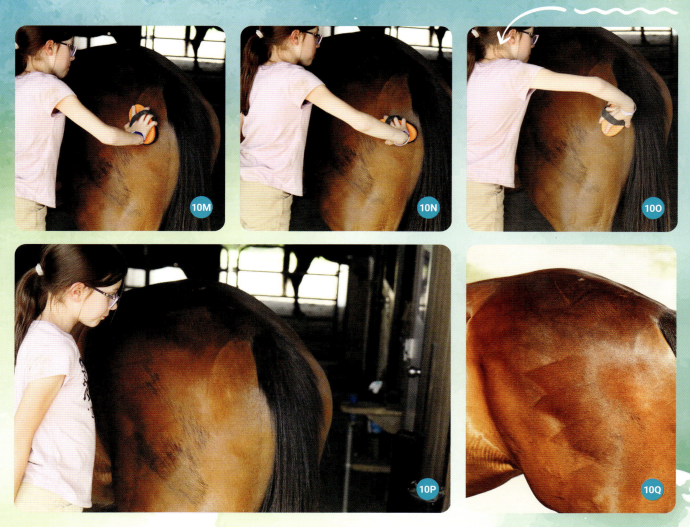

Shark Teeth

⭐ **10 A–Q** You can finish there or add shark teeth to make it extra special. Make sure not to touch what you have already done; any fingerprints will mess up the hair you have carefully placed. Place the brush on his hip, with the base of it pointed toward his hock **(A)**. Pull the brush on a straight line toward his hock **(B & C)**. Now, reposition your brush below the line you just made, this

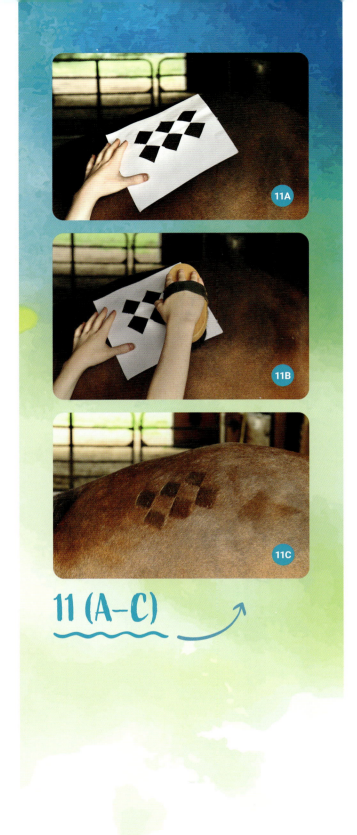

11 (A–C)

time pointing up toward the top of his tail **(D)**. Drag the brush following that line upward **(E & F)**. Pick your brush up and reposition it so it is on the same angle as step one, but below the lines you have made **(G)**. Drag the brush downward on that line **(H)**. Reposition the brush below the lines you have made, pointing up **(I)**. Drag the brush on that line **(J)**. Repeat these alternating steps until you hit the lower leg **(K & L)**. To finish the look, position your brush at the top of his tail. Then spin the top of the brush toward the ground **(M–O)**. This creates a circle over the muscle of his hindquarters **(P)**. The finished look! **(Q)**.

Stencils

Using a stencil is a great first step because it is easy. You can buy these from a tack shop or make your own using craft plastic sheets from the hobby store.

☆ **11 A–C** To do a stencil, brush all the hair on the horse's rump smooth. Then place the stencil parallel with his spine **(A)**. Being careful not to brush outside the stencil, brush the hair backward over the holes in the stencil **(B)**. Lift the stencil straight up without touching the hair, and admire your handiwork! **(C)**.

Stencil and Spray

You can also use a stencil and temporary color spray made to wash away easily to create fancy patterns. Use a spray made just for horses.

THE KID'S GUIDE TO HORSEMANSHIP AND GROOMING / Cat Hill & Emma Ford

12 (A–D)

☆ **12 A–D** First, brush the hair down so it's all going one direction. Then, have a helper hold the stencil in place for you **(A)**. Hold the spray a couple inches from the stencil and move it back and forth as you spray **(B)**. When it is windy, having a towel down helps prevent getting the spray outside the stencil **(C)**. You do not have to fill the whole stencil in—Beau looks great with just six diamonds **(D)**!

Braids

Braids are a fun way to turn your horse out looking his absolute best. The key to good braids is *braiding down*. To do a good job at this requires lots of practice, so braid whenever you can. You can practice braiding with yarn, bailing twine, or a friend's hair!

CHAPTER 10 / Pony Glow Up

13 (A–G)

Practicing

This is one of our favorite practice tools. Cut 30 or so pieces of yarn about the length of your arm. Tie them in a knot in the middle.

☆ **13 A–G** Now divide those pieces into three sections **(A)**. Start the braid by crossing the chunk of yarn on the right over the middle chunk **(B)**. Keeping your hands close to the knot, cross the left over the center **(C)**. Then cross the right over the center again **(D)**. Then the left over the center **(E)**. Keep alternating, right over center, left over center **(F)**. As you get better and better at it, the braid will get tighter and more even **(G)**. This is a great tool to practice on because you aren't attached to anything. If you can braid this, your pony will be happier because you won't be pulling down on his neck when you braid!

THE KID'S GUIDE TO HORSEMANSHIP AND GROOMING / Cat Hill & Emma Ford

Preparing Your Pony

Once you have the basic idea of braiding down, get your pony ready. Brush the mane out until it has no tangles.

☆ **14 A–C** You can use a little mousse, wax, or water on the mane. Put it in your hands **(A)**, then rub it down the mane **(B & C)**. Try different things and see what you like best, everyone is different.

Start Braiding Down

☆ **15 A–P (next page)** A braiding belt can be a great way to keep your tools at hand; otherwise, you will need pockets **(A)**. Use a small comb to separate out a small section of hair, three- or four- fingers-width **(B)**. Clip the hair back away from the hair you've separated **(C)**. Divide this section into three even pieces **(D–E)**. Take the hair from the right side over the middle piece **(F)**. Then take the hair from the left and cross over the middle **(G)**. Keep holding the sections as tight as you can by keeping your hands toward the top of the hair **(H)**. Alternate right over the middle, left over the middle as you go down the hair **(I & J)**. Use a rubber band to secure the end of the braid **(K–O)**. (Note that we are using a longer mane to demonstrate braiding down. Where you end the braid depends on the style of braid you are doing. Keep reading to find out how far down the hair to braid!) As you practice,

14 (A–C)

CHAPTER 10 / Pony Glow Up

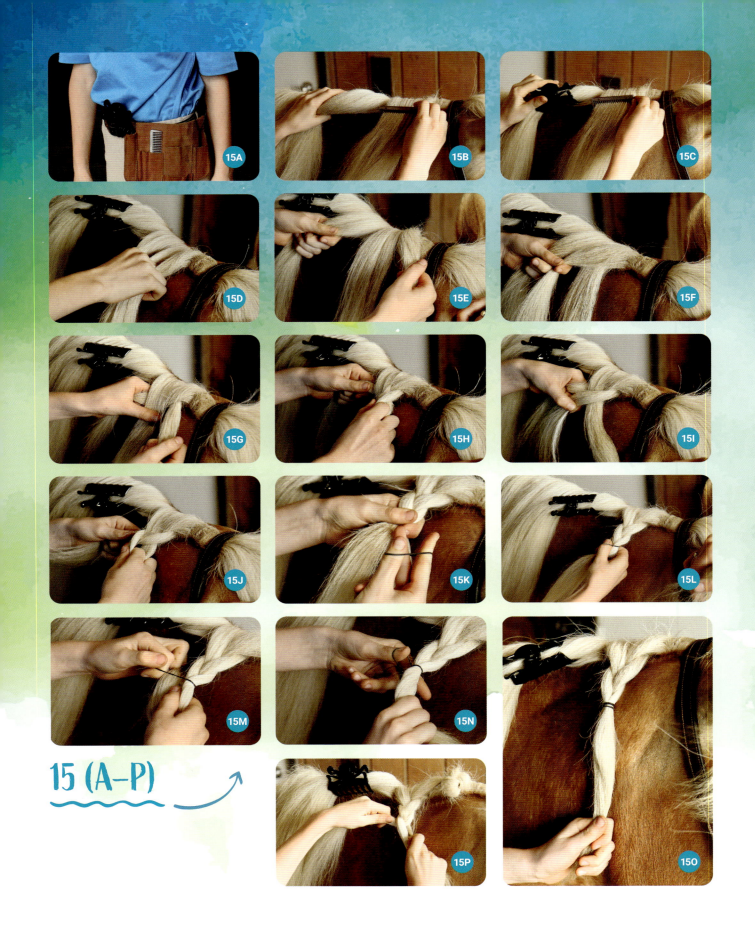

15 (A–P)

THE KID'S GUIDE TO HORSEMANSHIP AND GROOMING / Cat Hill & Emma Ford

keep trying to have the braid be snug by pulling the hair tight as you cross over **(P)**. Be careful not to pull down on the horse's neck. This can make him uncomfortable and then he will toss his head! Once you have practiced braiding down, it's time to pick which method to use to roll the braids up.

Rolling Braids for Short Manes

The *first* method is for manes that are pulled short. For this, you need braiding bands.

☆ **16 A–G** When braiding down for this method, you need to go all the way down to the bottom of the hair **(A)**, then twist up the end and secure with a rubber band **(B)**. Now think about halving the braid by folding the tip up. Take the bottom of the braid underneath and to the crest of the mane. Pinch it together with your thumb and forefinger **(C)**. Roll the braid in half again **(D)**. While using one hand to hold the "bun" together, use your free hand to wrap the band around the entire bun **(E)**. You will need to twist the band again to go around the bun **(F)**. If the bun unfolds, just take a second band, refold the braid, and wrap the

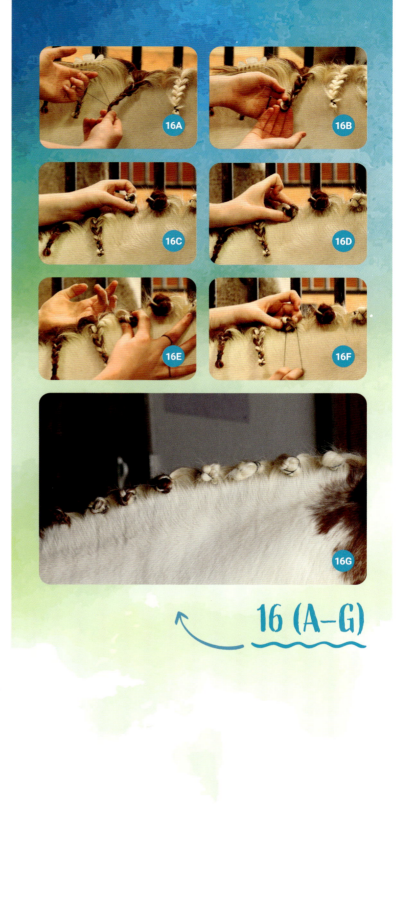

16 (A–G)

CHAPTER 10 / Pony Glow Up

155

17 (A–K)

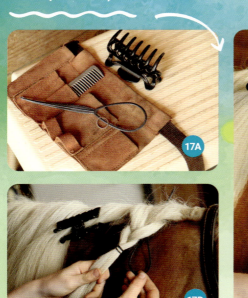
17A

17B

17C

17D

17E

17F

17H

17I

17G

17K

17J

THE KID'S GUIDE TO HORSEMANSHIP AND GROOMING / Cat Hill & Emma Ford

156

new band around it, making sure you catch the bottom of the braid as close to the crest as possible. When you are finished, you should have a line of similar sized, elegant braids on the top of the neck **(G)**.

Rolling Braids for Long Manes

The *second* method is great for horses and ponies with long manes.

☆**17 A–K** You will need a large plastic pull-through. These are sold at many grocery or pharmacy stores in the haircare section **(A)**. First, braid down about 4 to 5 inches, and rubber band the end **(B)**. Insert the pull-through pointy-end up from under the braid **(C & D)**. Pull the braid down through the loop of the pull-through **(E & F)**. Pull the pull-through up and the tail of the braid all the way through the base of the braid **(G & H)**. Using two rubber bands at a time **(I)**, grasp the braided bun and secure it with the bands **(J & K)**.

Connecting the Braids

☆**18 A–I** Move to the mane next to the braid you finished, and separate a bunch of hair. Divide this section

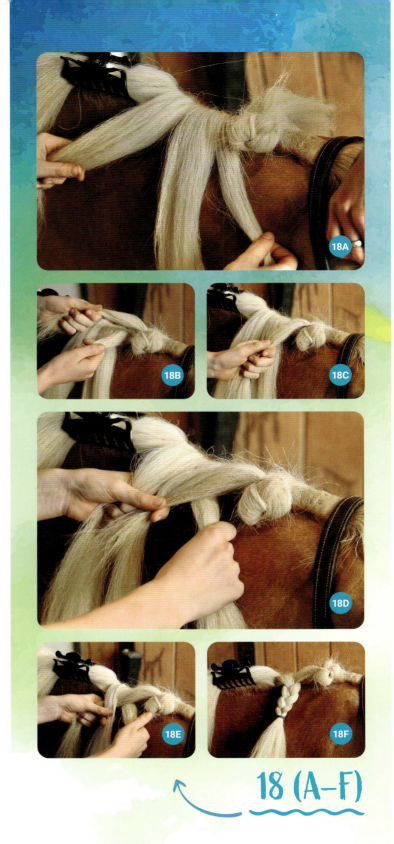

18 (A–F)

CHAPTER 10 / Pony Glow Up

157

18 (G–I)

into three pieces, with the piece closest to the braid a bit smaller than the others **(A)**. Pick up the tail of the old braid and the small section of hair from the new braid **(B)**. Join them together **(C)**, then start braiding down like normal **(D & E)**. Finish the braid at 4 to 5 inches down **(F)**. Pull this braid through just like the first **(G–I)**. Keep following this pattern all the way down the neck.

Ending Your Braid Pattern

☆ **19 A–E** On the last braid, braid farther down before banding the braid **(A)**. Pull the tail of the braid through itself to make a similar size bun **(B)**. Wrap the braid around the bun **(C)**, then rubber band it into place **(D)**. The finished product **(E)**.

A little note about braiding: It takes a long time and lots of practice to get braids just right. Do your best and be proud of the work you are doing. Every one of us professional grooms has had hundreds of messy braids before we could get the perfect ones you see us do at shows!

THE KID'S GUIDE TO HORSEMANSHIP AND GROOMING / Cat Hill & Emma Ford

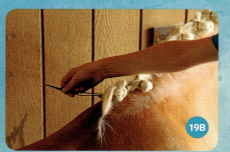

19 (A–E)

end of chapter 10

CHAPTER 10 / Pony Glow Up

159

chapter eleven

Professional Care

Professional Care

It takes a village to keep your pony happy and healthy. You are your pony's primary caretaker, but there are important needs that require specialists in their appropriate field. Veterinarians, farriers, and dentists are three extremely important professionals to help you keep on top of your pony's health throughout the year.

Veterinarian

Your veterinarian is someone who, ideally, you would only see twice a year. A veterinarian is a horse doctor. Your horse's routine visits will include a general checkup to catch anything you might miss, inoculations, and to pull your horses blood to do a Coggins test. However, ponies can and do get sick, lame, or hurt themselves throughout the year, so knowing your local horse vet and having his or her number easily accessible at the barn is paramount for good horse care.

Well Visits

These are the visits that include required "shots." Which ones are given to your pony is a decision your vet needs to make.

Across the United States and internationally, disease types and levels change.

A lot of you will remember having your shots for school. These are needed to prevent old illnesses, such as measles and smallpox, from returning. It is much the same for your pony. The required vaccinations are to prevent your pony from getting sick but also from transmitting the disease to others. Once you have decided what shots are needed, make sure you put future booster shots or six-month shots down in your Horse Care Diary.

These wellness visits are a good time for your pony to have his heart, lungs, and eyes checked to ensure all is in good shape.

☆ **1 A–E** You should plan on having your pony caught and ready for the vet **(A)**. An adult should always be in attendance, because even the best ponies sometimes don't like the vet. When your vet begins the examination, you should hold your pony, not have him on the cross-ties **(B)**. This helps prevent an accident should he get scared.

The veterinarian will check your pony all over, and while she does, you should be attentive to her and your pony **(C)**. If your pony doesn't like something, have your adult handler hold him, but stay close and listen to what the doctor has to say **(D)**. When the vet is using a stethoscope, she will need total quiet, so save your questions for later when she takes them out of her ears **(E)**. Even when your pony doesn't have

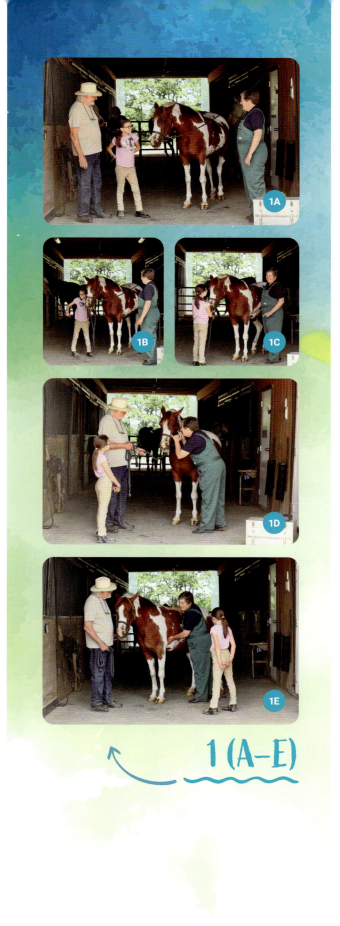

1 (A–E)

CHAPTER 11 / *Professional Care*

any outward signs of ill health, getting him checked can prevent a serious problem from starting.

Parasite control is extremely important because some worms can cause serious illness, weight loss, or even colic. Fecal counts are now considered a better way to prevent parasite infestation instead of a rotational worming program. Over the years, many parasites have become resistant to dewormers and are, therefore, ineffective. When your vet is coming for a wellness check, you need to take a small sample of your pony's manure and place it in a well-labeled Ziplock® bag. Ideally, the manure should be as fresh as possible to ensure fly eggs have not contaminated the sample. Give it to your vet and she can call you with the results normally within two days.

Urgent Care Visits

These visits can be for many issues, including swollen eyes, hives, coughing, mild colic, or a lameness. For these scenarios, you need to call your vet's practice and explain your problem as best as you can.

Signs of ill health could be, for example, your pony came in with a big cut on his left front leg or your pony starts coughing every time you start to ride him, or your pony's skin has funny bumps all over it.

It is very helpful to the vet if you can tell him your pony's *TPR*—this means *temperature, pulse,* and *respiration*. These three parameters, or *vital signs*, can signal to the vet how serious a problem might actually be.

Normal TPR ranges are affected by fitness level, air temperature, and the pony's natural temperament. It's important to practice taking a pony's TPR before he is sick, so here's how to do it.

Temperature

Every horse person needs to know how to check her horse's temperature. A horse's normal temperature is between 98 and 101 degrees Fahrenheit.

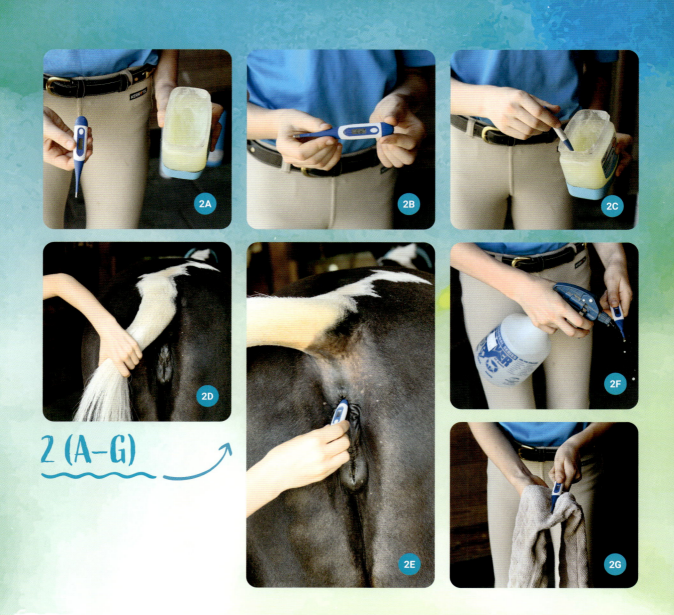

2 (A–G)

⭐ **2 A–G** To check a horse's temperature, we use a rectal thermometer and Vaseline® **(A)**. For the most accurate reading, a digital rectal thermometer works well. Check that it is on and working **(B)**. You will want to have a handler hold the horse's head while you take the horse's temperature. Put a little Vaseline on the thermometer to make it slippery—this helps prevent damage to the delicate tissues **(C)**. Stand to the side of your horse, and gently lift the tail up and to the side **(D)**. Then carefully insert the thermometer into the rectum **(E)**.

CHAPTER 11 / *Professional Care*

165

3 (A & B)

Wait, holding it carefully and paying attention to your horse's body language, until it beeps. Then remove the thermometer and step away from the hindquarters to read the screen. Once you have read the temperature, wash it off using a little alcohol **(F)**. Then towel it dry before storing it for the next time you need it **(G)**.

Pulse

The horse's pulse rate indicates how often the heart is pumping blood through the veins. A normal pulse rate is 30 to 40 beats per minute.

To take the pulse, you first need to find the large blood vessel that runs along the inside of the jaw (called the *transverse facial artery*).

Run your fingers (not your thumb) along the inside of the jaw until you feel a soft, rope-like object about the size of a pencil. You should be able to feel it move under the skin if you push against it. Very gently touch it with your pointer finger and push just hard enough to feel the artery.

☆ **3 A & B** If you go quiet and still, you should be able to feel the blood push against your fingertip in a rhythm. That is the horse's heartbeat. Once you have found it, count the beats for 15 seconds **(A)**, then multiply your number by 4, and the result is your horse's pulse rate! Sometimes it can be very difficult to feel the transverse facial artery because you cannot see it. You can also use the *temporal artery*. This is a smaller, often clearly visible vein near the horse's eye. It is easy to squish

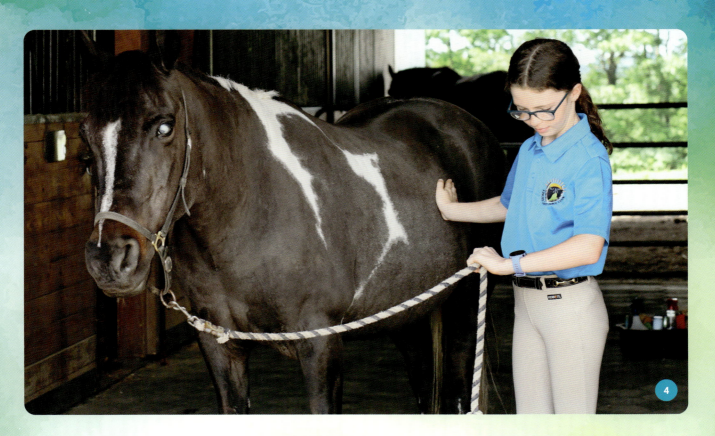

and turn off, so place your pointer and middle finger on it gently until you can feel the bump of the blood pushing up on your fingertips **(B)**.

Respiration

A horse's respiration rate refers to how many breaths he takes in a minute. A resting respiration rate should be 8 to 14 breaths per minute. To count this, you will want to watch the flanks carefully for 15 seconds, then multiply your number by 4, just like for finding the pulse. For example, if you count three breaths in 15 seconds, your horse's respiration rate is 12.

☆**4** It may help to put a hand on your horse's flank to feel the rise and fall of his breath.

Lameness

Another urgent care visit is when your horse is lame. Lameness simply means that he isn't carrying his weight evenly on all his legs. A horse can be a little lame, or very, very lame and unable to put one foot down at all.

When your vet is coming out for a lameness exam, you will need to be able to "trot up" for the exam. To do this, you need to walk in a straight line away from the vet, turn and walk straight back toward her. Then the veterinarian will ask you to do the same at the trot.

☆**5 A–C (next page)** To trot a straight line, pick something to look at—a fence post or tree—and run straight toward that tree with a loose lead rope

CHAPTER 11 / Professional Care

5 (A–C)

(A). Turn your pony around and trot him straight back toward the vet **(B)**. Looking down can make you lose track of your horse, and then the vet can't watch his legs properly **(C)**. You may hear your vet give the lameness a "grade." "One" is slightly lame, and "five" is unable to stand on the leg. Lots of not-so-serious things can make your horse lame, so don't panic—just listen and ask questions.

Emergency Care

These calls are the ones you hope you never have to make. It normally means you have found your pony in a very uncomfortable situation. Anything from being non-weight-bearing on a leg, to rolling aggressively in his stall or paddock, to bleeding a lot from a major gash.

In these situations, never put yourself in harm's way. Ask an adult to call your vet and report an emergency and explain what you are seeing. If your pony seems quiet, you should try and keep him calm, and take him into a well-lit location so that the vet can observe and assess the situation when she arrives.

If your pony is not weight-bearing, which means not using one of his legs at all, do not move him. If it's cold, ask an adult to find a blanket to keep him warm while waiting for the vet.

When your pony is rolling aggressively, ask an adult to help you get a halter on. Start walking your pony; continued rolling can lead to a twisted gut or injured legs, so the walking helps keep the pony's mind off his pain.

THE KID'S GUIDE TO HORSEMANSHIP AND GROOMING / Cat Hill & Emma Ford

Do NOT enter the stall of an upset, hurt, or scared pony without experienced help.

Farrier

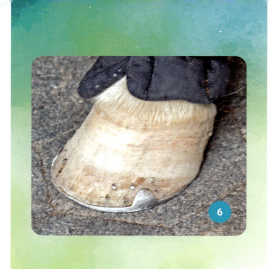

How often you see your farrier is dependent on a few factors: Does your pony wear shoes? Or is he barefoot? How many days a week does he work, and how hard does he work when he is ridden? What are his living conditions, turnout schedule, and diet?

Most ponies need to have a visit from the farrier every four to eight weeks. Once you find a schedule that works for your pony, try to maintain it. Going over the usual timing can lead to lameness. It's a good idea to schedule the next visit from the farrier while he is at your barn. This makes it easy to make sure you don't get off track.

When your pony is barefoot, you need to watch out for cracking of the hoof wall. Left unchecked, these cracks can turn into painful problems.

If shod, you need to become aware of how the shoe is fitted, and notice when your pony starts to grow over the shoe, when nail clinches start to rise, and when the shoe has shifted or become "sprung."

☆ **6** Here we see a hoof at the end of the shoeing cycle. Look at the back of the shoe, how the heel has spread out and over the shoe, and how long the toe looks. When your farrier arrives, have your pony already inside with dry, picked-out feet and clean legs.

☆ **7** Don't put hoof oil on before he does the feet, though! It's a sure way to annoy the farrier because now he will get that hoof oil all over him.

CHAPTER 11 / Professional Care

PRO TIP
Ask Your Farrier

Be sure to ask your farrier for recommendations of what hoof oil to apply throughout the year. As weather conditions change, how dry, wet, or brittle the hooves become will change as well.

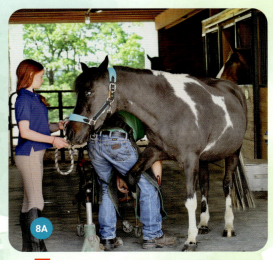

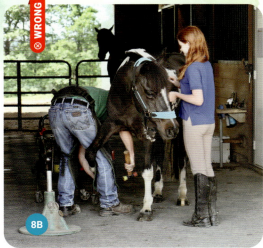

★ **8 A & B** Plan on holding your pony during the farrier's visit to make sure he behaves. Hold the pony on the same side as the farrier is working **(A)**, instead of the opposite side **(B)**. If Stormy acted up, Gwen would pull the lead rope, and Stormy would swing her body toward our farrier Russ, putting him in danger.

★ **9 A & B** Never have your phone out when holding a horse for the farrier—you can get everyone involved hurt because you aren't paying attention **(A)**. Don't let chatting distract you either. Stormy thinks about giving Russ a nip while the girls are distracted **(B)**.

Shoeing Procedure

★ **10 A–K (page 172)** If your horse wears shoes, the farrier will start by removing the nails **(A & B)**, then the shoe **(C)**. He will trim the hoof to shape using nippers and a file **(D & E)**. Then he will heat the shoe up in a small, hot stove, and use an anvil and hammer to shape it to the same shape as

THE KID'S GUIDE TO HORSEMANSHIP AND GROOMING / Cat Hill & Emma Ford

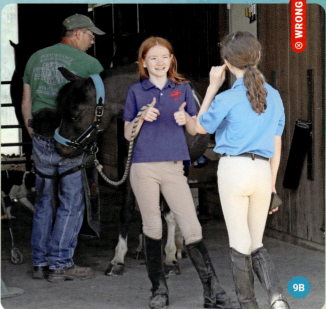

9 (A & B)

your horse's foot **(F)**. He will then check the fit by putting it on the horse's foot while still hot **(G)**. This might smell funny and be very smoky, but your horse doesn't feel any pain. Although, especially when they are new to being shod, some horses might need a reassuring pat to let them know the smoke won't hurt them. Once the fit is just right, the farrier will use a hammer to put nails into the outside wall of the hoof. This area of the hoof doesn't feel anything either, so it doesn't hurt them **(H)**. He will then stretch the horse's leg out in front of him and put it on a stand while he trims off the sharp ends of the nails **(I)**, and uses a rasp to smooth the ends so the pony doesn't hurt himself with them **(J)**. Notice that Ella moved to the other side to hold the horse so she is out of the way. He may finish by putting a coat of oil or paint over the hoof **(K)**. If your horse doesn't wear shoes, the farrier will simply use the nippers and rasp to trim and shape the hoof.

CHAPTER 11 / *Professional Care*

10 (A–K)

THE KID'S GUIDE TO HORSEMANSHIP AND GROOMING / Cat Hill & Emma Ford

172

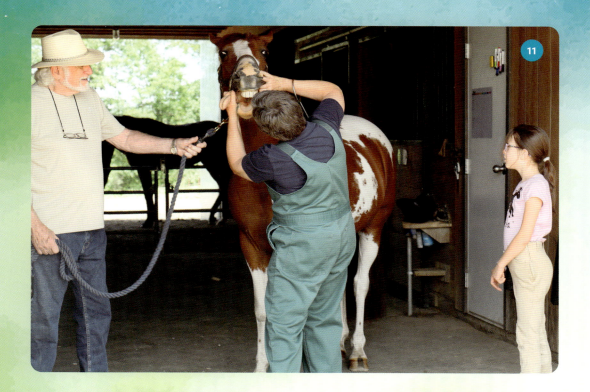

Horse Dentist

Ponies' teeth should be checked at least once a year. Younger ponies might need to have their teeth done more often as baby teeth are lost and adult teeth come in. If you notice your pony struggling to chew hay or grain, or if he suddenly becomes fussy in the bridle, having a dentist check his mouth would be a good call.

Ponies chew in a sideways motion, which over time creates sharp points on the edges of their teeth. If not filed down, these edges cause sore ulcers in the sides of the mouth.

☆11 Your vet may do dental work, too, so if you do not have a specific dentist, ask your vet to check your pony's teeth when she comes to do your wellness exams.

CHAPTER 11 / Professional Care

Caring for the Village

When we talk about the "village" that helps care for your horse or pony, it's really important to always be respectful and kind. Saying thank you goes a long way, so say it often, and mean it. Without the support of your team, you cannot ride and enjoy your pony!

While we are on the topic, make sure to thank your parents or adults that make it possible for you to go to the barn and who pay the bills for you. It's easy to forget that without them, horses are a faraway dream!

Life with horses is very rewarding. Unlike many other sports and activities, you get to have a relationship with another species. The friendship of a horse is different than any other. Taking the best care possible of him allows you to develop deep bonds and lasting friendships.

As you get older, you should learn from many expert horse people how to improve your relationship with your equine friend as well as improve your riding skills. Every professional you meet started as a horse-crazy kid who loved the horses—just like you.

Our first book, *World Class Grooming for Horses,* is a great next step in the very best in horse management once you feel ready to learn more.

The Ponies and Horse Kids in This Book

We cannot say thank you enough to both the
Finger Lakes Pony Club, for donating children,
and to the Treacys at Cal's Legacy Acres
for donating both kind, patient horses
and a lovely venue to hold our photograph shoots.
Without them, this book would not have been possible!

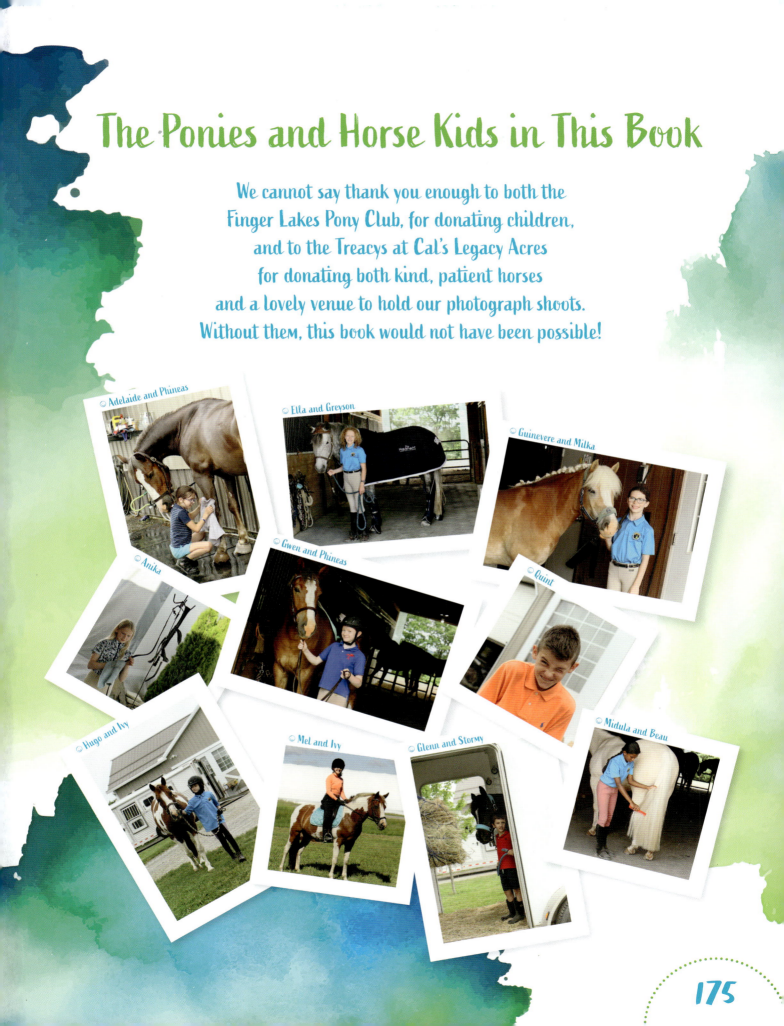

175

Learn More!

Contact professional grooms
Cat Hill and Emma Ford
about their educational clinics for all ages:

www.WorldClassGrooming.com

f @worldclassgroomingforhorses

◉ @worldclassgrooming

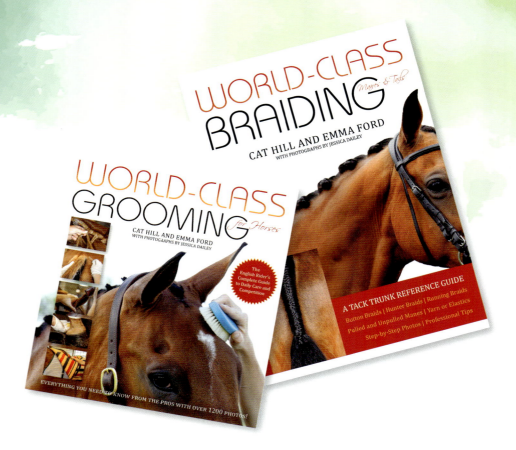